Becoming a Strategic Thinker

Developing Skills for Success

W. James Potter

University of California at Santa Barbara

PEARSON

Prentice
Hall

Upper Saddle River, New Jersey
Columbus, Ohio

Library of Congress Cataloging-in-Publication Data

Potter, W. James.
   Becoming a strategic thinker: developing skills for success / W. James Potter
      p. cm.
   Includes bibliographical references and index.
   ISBN 0-13-117983-7
  1. Critical thinking. I. Title.

B809.2.P68 2005
153.4'2—dc22   2004018108

Vice President and Publisher: Jeffery W. Johnston
Senior Acquisitions Editor: Sande Johnson
Assistant Editor: Erin Anderson
Production Editor: Holcomb Hathaway
Design Coordinator: Diane C. Lorenzo
Cover Designer: Ali Mohrman
Cover Art: Ali Mohrman
Production Manager: Susan Hannahs
Director of Marketing: Ann Castel Davis
Marketing Manager: Amy Judd
Compositor: Carlisle Communications, Ltd.

13 2022

Pearson Prentice Hall™ is a trademark of Pearson Education, Inc.
Pearson® is a registered trademark of Pearson plc
Prentice Hall® is a registered trademark of Pearson Education, Inc.

Pearson Education Ltd.
Pearson Education Singapore Pte. Ltd.
Pearson Education Canada, Ltd.
Pearson Education–Japan

Pearson Education Australia Pty. Limited
Pearson Education North Asia Ltd.
Pearson Educación de Mexico, S.A. de C.V.
Pearson Education Malaysia Pte. Ltd.

ISBN 0-13-117983-7

Brief Contents

Contents

CHAPTER

6

Skill 3: Induction   85

CHAPTER

7

Skill 4: Deduction   99

CHAPTER **10**

Skill 7: Abstracting   141

CHAPTER **11**

Skill 8: Persuasive Expression   153

CHAPTER **Springboard   165**

12

Preface

Have any of the following things ever happened to you?

- You are in a course and nothing seems to make sense to you. You just can't seem to get started learning the material.
- You spend many hours reading an assigned book or article, yet when you finish it you can't remember much of anything important that you just read.
- You study much more than other students, yet you earn lower grades than they do.
- When you hand in an exam, you are confident that you knew all the material that was tested, and you are convinced you have earned a good grade. But when you get the graded exam back, you see that points are marked off, and you did not do nearly as well as you expected.
- When your professor goes over the answers you wrote on a test, you are frustrated because you feel you knew the material but were not able to express it well in your answers.

We all have experienced these things from time to time. Education is a continuing challenge, and at times students may get frustrated that they are not learning much, especially when they are working hard. If these experiences happen more than you would like them to, then you need to take some steps so that they won't continue to occur in the future. The best way to position yourself so that you will encounter more rewarding experiences instead of frustrating ones is to become a *strategic thinker.*

Strategic thinkers are people who are able to make good decisions quickly about which information is most important and which can be ignored. They are able to catalog information in their mind effectively so they can retrieve it when they need it. Strategic thinkers are able to see the big picture—about the world, their place in it, and how education will improve their place. With all this as context, they know how to transform information into knowledge effectively and efficiently.

This book is not going to teach you how to think. You already know how to do that. You have made many good decisions and accomplished much already. You have significant abilities or you would not be in college. But you can always get better—if you did not believe that you could strengthen your abilities even more, then you would not have made the sacrifice to enroll in college.

My goal with this book is to help you understand how *you can **think better** by becoming a strategic thinker*. You will strengthen your ability to reason more *effectively* for yourself and depend less on the media and other people telling you what to think. You will learn to think more *efficiently* so that you can get greater rewards for the same amount of effort you have been putting into your courses. By becoming a strategic thinker, you will be able to solve problems in course assignments as well as in life more quickly and with more confidence.

HOW TO BECOME A STRATEGIC THINKER

In order to become a strategic thinker, you need two things. First, you need some *guidance;* second, you need *commitment* to working on exercises that will strengthen your skills and build up your knowledge structures. This book will help you with both of these tasks.

In the chapters ahead, you will develop a set of eight skills that are the core tools for strategic thinking. In Chapter 1, you will see how strategic thinking is a powerful way to meet the challenges presented by the flood of information in our culture and in higher education. In Chapter 2, you will see that there is a core set of eight skills that strategic thinkers use as their primary tools when they encounter information and try to make sense of it. You will also learn how these skills are used to build knowledge structures. In Chapter 3, you will find out what your current knowledge style is and learn how to work from your basic knowledge style to become more of a strategic thinker.

The next eight chapters present each of the eight skills of strategic thinking. They will help you develop each strategic thinking skill more fully and give you exercises so you can practice what you are learning.

The book ends with a chapter that presents a springboard for developing the eight skills. You will see how to begin with your natural knowledge style, then work from your strengths to overcome your weaknesses in order to develop a more useful knowledge style.

This book can open doors of understanding for you. But you must do your part. You need to consider carefully the ideas in each chapter, then incorporate those ideas into your own approach to information. Also, you will need to do the exercises presented in the eight skill chapters. Skills are like muscles—they need to be exercised in order to get stronger. No matter how strong your skills are, you can make them even stronger. The more you work with them, the stronger they get. But if you give up working with them, they will get weaker. Exercising is the only way to improve them.

Developing the eight skills requires an investment of effort from you. In the beginning, it may be difficult to get into the habit of doing the exercises. But when you commit to investing your time and effort to strengthen your skills, you will start down a road toward rewards that will more than pay back all your effort. Improvement may be slow at first, but if you keep investing your effort, the improvements will come faster. Once you start noticing the improvements, the exercises will seem easier, and the rewards will accelerate.

The rewards from your investment of time and energy in developing as a strategic thinker will continue beyond this course. Because the strategic-thinking core skills apply to all bodies of knowledge, these skills can help you work with information and solve problems in any type of course. And even more important, you can use the skills outside of your college courses, in your everyday life—to solve problems about friends and make better decisions about how to spend your time and money. Also, the more you develop this set of eight skills, the more successful you can be in any career beyond college. With stronger strategic-thinking skills, you will be more competitive for jobs in the most interesting and satisfying careers. Without these skills, however, you are limiting yourself to low-level jobs. For example, in the retail sales career path, if your skill set is limited to memorization, you can hold only a clerk-type position. Once hired, you will be given a list of procedures to memorize, such as how to run the cash register, how to stock the shelves, and how to put prices on the merchandise. You will do these things over and over. If instead you have a strong set of strategic-thinking skills, you can take on much more challenging—and interesting—tasks that may be different every day. You might be asked to determine what the prices of merchandise should be and when to put certain items on sale, to suggest changes in the layout of the store, and to train new employees. You need to demonstrate a greater skill set before you will be given these types of responsibilities.

Think about what kind of a career you want to have, and ask yourself if you are developing the kind of skills that would prepare you for the "clerk" level or the "professional" level in that career. If you are interested in a career in medicine, would you prefer to dispense pills and treatments that others have prescribed, or would you rather diagnose people's problems and develop treatments? If you are interested in a career in law, would you prefer to check facts and type up other people's arguments, or would you rather construct your own arguments? If a professional career is what you want, then you need to develop a strong set of skills that help you filter out useless or bad information, filter in good information, and transform that good information into knowledge that can solve challenging problems. Once you have developed this set of skills, you are better able to think like a professional, regardless of the field—medicine, law, business, architecture, teaching, engineering, writing, science, and so on.

The ability to think strategically delivers many kinds of rewards, both in college courses and in the world outside academia. The earlier you develop this ability, the sooner you can start experiencing the many rewards.

Acknowledgments

I have been teaching the ideas in this book for two decades. During that time, I have learned so much from my students at Western Michigan University, Florida State University, Indiana University, UCLA, Stanford University, and now at the University of California at Santa Barbara. These many students have shown me what skills they needed to be successful in reading, thinking, arguing, writing papers, and taking exams.

I would like to thank the following reviewers, who offered constructive suggestions for improving this book: Norma Jeanne Campbell, Fayetteville State University; Christina Chapman, Lewis and Clark Community College; Dan King, Colorado Christian University; Kathleen Riepe, University of Wisconsin–Parkside; Marybeth Ruscica, St. John's University; Carolyn Brooks-Harris, University of Hawaii–Manoa; Kathryn Jarvis, Auburn University; and Judith Lynch, Kansas State University.

I also thank the many talented people at Prentice Hall who helped me shape the ideas into a text. I am especially grateful to Sande Johnson—and her able assistant Erin Anderson—who showed an early interest in this project, then guided and encouraged me every step along the way. Also, thanks to the reviewers of earlier versions of this manuscript. Because of the blind review process, I don't know your names, but I have greatly valued your input. Last, but definitely not least, I thank a special reviewer: my daughter Molly, who carefully read every word of the manuscript when she was preparing to go off to her freshman year of college. Molly pointed out many places where I needed to increase clarity, decrease corniness, and avoid boring the readers. I have tried my best to meet Molly's high standards for crystal-clear, exciting, non-corny nirvana, but since I am not 19 years old and this is not a rock concert, I have fallen short of that lofty standard. Even so, this book is a lot better than it would have been without Molly's insights. Thank you!

The Challenges

LEARNING OBJECTIVES

By reading this chapter, you will:

1. Develop an appreciation for how much information is flooding our society.
2. Learn that surviving and prospering in this information-flooded society requires that you meet two challenges:

   - The challenge of filtering information, and

   - The challenge of using information.

3. Understand that becoming a strategic thinker is the best way to meet the information challenges effectively and efficiently.

W e are all being flooded with information constantly. This presents us with two major challenges. The first challenge is making good filtering decisions. We must figure out how to ignore almost all the information, without overlooking that small percentage of information that could really help us. The second challenge is to use the information we select for our own purposes. The goal of a good education is to help us function and succeed in our information-saturated society by meeting these two fundamental challenges.

This book will help you with both of these major challenges in life and in education. It will help by showing you how to become a strategic thinker. **Strategic thinking** is an active and optimistic approach to learning. Strategic thinkers are aware of challenges and eagerly encounter them, because they are excited by the challenges and confident in their abilities, not just to meet the challenges but to *excel*. Strategic thinking is a perspective that guides people into making good decisions about what information to seek and how to get the most out of that information.

In this chapter it will become clear to you why these challenges of filtering and using information are so important and why they should be the focus of your college education. In the next chapter, you will learn how you can meet these challenges by becoming a strategic thinker.

Strategic thinking
Perspective that guides learners in making good decisions about what information to seek and how to get the most out of that information.

INFORMATION SATURATION

W e are overwhelmed by information (see Figure 1.1). For example, this year in the United States alone, approximately 65,000 book titles will be published. Throughout the world, radio stations will send out 65.5 million hours of original programming this year, and television stations will add another 48 million hours of programming. Hollywood film studios will release one major film every day, on average, and those studios make available another 169,500 television programs in their archives. Ten thousand magazines are published in this country. In addition, the World Wide Web offers access to about 2.5 *billion* documents. These are only the publicly available pages, referred to as the surface

Figure 1.1   Information vehicles.

Medium	United States	World
Books (titles per year)	64,711	968,735
Radio Stations	12,600	43,973
TV Broadcast Stations	1,884	33,071
Newspapers	2,386	22,643
Mass Market Periodicals	20,000	80,000
Scholarly Journals	10,500	40,000
Newsletters	10,000	40,000
Archived Office Pages	3×10^9	7.5×10^9

Information is from Lyman & Varian, 2001.

Web. There is also what is called the deep Web, which consists of pages that require memberships or fees or that are otherwise private. The deep Web has been estimated to be 400 to 550 times the size of the surface Web (Lyman & Varian, 2001).

There is a huge amount of information in our society—and the amount of information is increasing at a rapid rate. In 1984, Peter Large computed that more information had been produced in the 30-year period after 1954 than in the 5,000 years before that date (Large, 1984). Writing in *Megatrends,* John Naisbett estimated that, in the early 1980s, scientific and technical information was doubling every 5.5 years and that, by the 1990s, this rate would accelerate to a doubling of information every 20 months. As startling as these figures are, they are likely to be hopelessly outdated as estimates of the speed of information generation in 2004, because half of all the scientists who have ever lived on earth are alive today and producing information.

It is impossible for an individual to keep up with all this information. For example, if you were to try to read only the new books published this year, you would have to read a book every 8 minutes for 24 hours each day with no breaks over the entire year. All that effort would be needed just to keep up with the new titles published in only this one country! You would have no time left to read any of the other 66 million book titles in existence worldwide. Also, if you wanted to watch all the television programming broadcast in this year alone, it would take you about 550 *centuries*—if you took no breaks!

We live in an environment that is far different from any environment humans have ever experienced before. And the environment changes at an ever increasing pace—the result of the accelerating generation of information and the sharing of that information through the increasing number of media channels. Messages are being delivered to everyone, everywhere, constantly. We are all saturated with information.

Is this a hopeless situation? For many people it seems to be. Many people feel so overwhelmed with information that they put their minds on a kind of automatic pilot and ignore all information. Other people define their world very narrowly and only deal with information on a tiny sliver of topics. A few people try to broaden themselves and explore a wider range of what life has to offer; these people typically enroll in colleges in order to sample the broad scope of human thinking and find out what kinds of ideas appeal to them most.

The college experience, however, can often feel like an overwhelming journey through information. This can be especially true during the first two years of a liberal arts program, where you will encounter a great deal of material across a wide range of subjects—physical sciences, social sciences, humanities, and the arts. You will be asked to study long works of fiction, dense texts of technical terms and formulas, unfamiliar theories about human thinking and behavior, and works of art across many different cultures. You will be expected to make sense of all this in order to learn how the world operates and where your place is in it.

How can you navigate through all the information in a way that will allow you to experience the variety of human thought, but at the same time keep from being overwhelmed? You can do it by becoming a strategic thinker—by learning to handle the two major challenges of information: filtering information and using it to solve problems.

THE CHALLENGE OF FILTERING INFORMATION

We cannot possibly process all the information available, nor can we attend to more than a very small percentage of it. But we cannot ignore all the information, because there is a great deal that can help us in major ways—to get good jobs and construct meaningful careers; to understand what it means to be human and find our place in the world; and to help us build relationships with friends, family members, and significant others. For most of us in everyday life, the challenge of filtering information is met by automatically filtering almost all of it out of our conscious awareness. That is, we simply ignore almost all of it.

You probably are not aware of how much you depend on your mind to filter out information automatically, without your even thinking about it. Consider what takes place when you go to a supermarket to do your grocery shopping. Let's say you spend 20 minutes in the store and buy 50 items. How many decisions did you make while shopping? 50 decisions? No, you made 30,000 decisions—because that is the number of brands and products on the shelves of a typical supermarket. When you decided to buy your 50 items, you also decided *not* to buy the other 29,950 brands and products. How was it possible that you could have made 30,000 decisions in 20 minutes? You put your mind on automatic pilot to filter out the 29,950 brands and products you did not buy. Your mind did this automatically, with no effort from you. This automatic filtering allows us to make thousands of decisions in a very short period of time and thus get through our many tasks each day reasonably efficiently. However, this efficiency has a downside: automatic filtering is likely to filter out many things that we should attend to. For example, if you had taken the time to look at the prices of the brands competing with the brands you bought, you would likely have been able to save money. If you are health conscious and had spent more time looking at the labels of many more brands and products, you would likely have left the store with more nutritious foods.

Students often use automatic filtering in their college courses. For example, the typical textbook may have 120,000 words, yet after you have finished reading it, can you remember reading all of those words, or even a small fraction of them? A professor who lectures in a course will typically utter about 12,000 words in a 50-minute class, but you do not record all those words in your notes—that would require about 60 pages of handwriting per class meeting. Clearly, you filter when you read the text and listen to lectures in class. We must filter. There is no way around it. The question is not whether we should filter. Instead, the question is: Are we making good filtering decisions? Are we attending to the right information?

In some college courses, especially introductory courses, professors will do much of the filtering for you. They provide handouts of important terms, outlines of the lectures, and study guides for the exams. Even with these "high-direction" professors, you still need to make many decisions for yourself. For example, not everything on the study guide is equally important. Professors rarely test every single item listed on a study guide, so you must decide which elements are more important, that is, which elements are most likely to be on the exam. Also, professors are not in a position to determine which information is most likely to be useful in the students' lives. Each student is different, so each student must make these decisions for herself.

In many courses, especially the more advanced ones, professors transfer the responsibility of making decisions about what material is most important to the student. These are courses where many books and articles are assigned, and students must read hundreds of pages each week. You must decide which of the readings are the most important in order to read them more carefully; you must decide which to skim, and which you can risk ignoring. The same decisions must be made—although on a smaller scale—when you are reading an article or a book chapter; you must decide which parts of the article are most important, which parts you can skim, and which you can ignore.

If you do not make these decisions well, you are likely to miss the point of the course and suffer the consequences with a low grade or poor understanding. Or, if you refuse to make these decisions at all, you will be forced to treat every word in every sentence of every paragraph on every page in every chapter of every book as equally important. Studying like this would doom you to spending so much time with the readings that you would soon fall hopelessly behind in the course.

It is natural that students look to their professors for help in filtering information in a course. However, there are two kinds of help—immediate and long term. Immediate help is what students typically want, but long-term help is what they need. You have probably heard the saying that goes: *Give a hungry man some rice and you will help him with his hunger today; give the man a plow and you will help him with his hunger for life.* College is more about helping you learn to plow the fields of information and make your own decisions. Professors who make all the filtering decisions for their students will make those students happy in the short term—but when you are put in a position to have to strengthen your abilities to filter for yourself, you will learn far more from the course.

THE CHALLENGE OF USING INFORMATION TO SOLVE PROBLEMS

The second challenge in every college course is doing something with the information. For many students this "doing something" is limited to memorizing—holding facts in their mind long enough to be able to recall them on a test. This may be fine in introductory courses where you must learn the main ideas, definitions, and lists in an area. For example, in an introduction to a foreign language, you must memorize words, their pronunciation, and their meaning. But once you have a basic working knowledge of a language, you must use it. This means you cannot continue to repeat the sentences you have memorized in the texts; instead, you must move on to use the language to express your own ideas.

"Using" Information

The skill of memorizing is indeed essential, and it may be sufficient to do well in introductory courses where your primary task is to retain names, dates, lists, and definitions of terms. However, almost all courses in college will require you to do more with the information and to demonstrate that you have learned (not just

Information

Content of messages; may be facts, opinions, pictures, sounds, etc.

Messages

Vehicles that deliver information to us. Messages can be delivered by many different media— television, radio, CDs, video games, books, newspapers, Web sites, conversations, lectures, concerts, signs along the streets, labels on the products we buy, and so on.

Facts

Discrete bits of information, such as names (of people, places, characters, events, etc.), definitions of terms, formulae, lists, and the like. A fact is something raw, unprocessed, and context free.

Knowledge

Information that has been processed to give it more meaning and context than bits of information or facts.

memorized) the material. Professors will ask you to use the material to solve problems: to analyze arguments, evaluate the worth of those arguments, create your own informed opinions, project trends into the future, and recognize patterns across bodies of information. To accomplish these more involved tasks, you will need many more skills in addition to the ability to memorize.

At this point, I need to make a distinction among some key terms—information, messages, knowledge, and facts. **Information** is that which is delivered to us in **messages;** it is the content of those messages. Messages can be delivered by many different media—television, radio, CDs, video games, books, newspapers, Web sites, conversations, lectures, concerts, signs along the streets, labels on the products we buy, and so on. They can be large (an entire Hollywood movie) or small (one utterance by a character in a movie). They can be complex (a philosopher's metaphysical position laid out in a dense book) or simple (a common word).

Many messages are composed of facts. A **fact** is something raw, unprocessed, and context free. For example, when you watch the news and hear messages about terrorism, those messages are composed of facts, such as "The World Trade Center in New York City was destroyed on September 11, 2001." "On that day, the United States declared war on terrorism." "The person suspected of planning the attack on the World Trade Center was Osama bin Laden." These statements are facts. Facts are discrete bits of information, such as names (of people, places, characters, events, etc.), definitions of terms, formulae, lists, and the like. Facts by themselves are not knowledge any more than a pile of bricks is a house. **Knowledge** requires structure. The facts need to be evaluated for their individual quality, then arranged into a useful design. This structure displays what is most important and how facts are related to one another. Strategic thinking helps people build knowledge structures that are accurate and useful.

When we talk about "using" information, what does that mean? When a person uses information, he goes beyond the absorption of facts, definitions, and lists to transform the information into something relevant to his own experience to achieve his own goals. Essentially it is problem solving, and college is essentially an experience of problem solving. If you are good at solving all kinds of problems, you will do well in college and enjoy the experience of learning. But if you do not understand the nature of problems or if you do not have good problem-solving skills, you will struggle.

College presents all kinds of problems. A common problem is understanding what you are reading. In almost every class, you will be asked to read some texts, and you must figure out which words and ideas in those text are the most important. Another common problem is organizing information. Most classes will ask you to assemble information from several different lectures, discussions, and readings to arrive at higher-level insights. Another common problem is expressing what you have learned. In many courses, you will be asked to write essays; you must decide which ideas to highlight, how to sequence those ideas, and how to support each idea with evidence and argumentation.

In college, as in everyday life, the problems you encounter can be grouped into two categories. One category includes problems that are *fully specified*. The other category includes problems that are missing key information; this type of problem is referred to as *partially specified.*

Fully Specified Problems

Some problems in college are relatively easy to solve. When the professor clearly provides a full set of steps to a solution, and when you understand each step, reaching a solution is simple. Consider the following problem:

$$6 + 18 = \underline{\hspace{1cm}}$$

If you understand that "6" and "18" represent numbers with particular values and that the symbol "+" means addition, then you can arrive at a solution of 24 with ease and have confidence that your solution is correct. This is what is called a **fully specified problem,** because you have enough information to solve the problem.

Partially Specified Problems

Not all problems are fully specified. Some are partially specified. For example, consider the following problem:

$$Y + Z = 24$$

This problem has two unknowns (Y and Z), so there is not enough information to arrive at one solution with confidence. You could answer 6 and 18, while I might answer 12 and 12, and we would both be correct. There are also many other correct answers to this problem, because it is only **partially specified.** To most of us, each of these answers intuitively seems faulty. If so many answers are possible, can any one of them be regarded as THE solution? We prefer a more fully specified problem, such as $5 + Z = 24$; with this problem, we have enough information to know that Z is 19. There is one and only one correct answer.

With fully specified problems, we can memorize the answer or we can learn the process to solve the problem. Both approaches work well. However, with partially specified problems, there is no way to memorize an answer, and we cannot learn specific steps to arrive at a particular "right" answer. The box on the following page offers more information on recognizing partially specified problems.

It is tempting to regard partially specified problems as "trick questions." They seem to be unfair in some way. Perhaps you have sometimes felt that professors are not doing their job if they ask you to solve a problem without explicitly giving you all the information you need to solve it. Perhaps you have avoided courses that pose such problems and instead looked for courses where the professor clearly tells you everything that is important in the readings and gives you detailed study guides so you know everything that will be on an exam. These professors have translated all their course material into simple, fully specified problems. Introductory courses are often presented in this way. Problems posed on exams take the form of:

- Who is the father of psychoanalysis?
- In what year did Charles Dickens publish *The Christmas Carol*?
- Define the economic principle of "economy of scale."
- From the U. S. Constitution, list the steps in the process of a bill becoming a law.

Each of these problems is fully specified, and each has one correct answer.

Fully specified problem
A task where you are given enough information to solve the problem completely and arrive at one and only one correct solution.

Partially specified problem
A task where there is not enough information in the problem to guide you to one and only one correct solution.

How to Recognize Partially Specified Problems

Look for one of these characteristics:

1. No standard criteria to sanction one solution as the "best" solution to the problem
   - Several people could each construct a different solution to the problem, and there is no way to determine which is the best solution.
   - **Example:** Ann looks at the problem A + B = 8 and knows that there are many possible solutions, such as A is 1 and B is 7; A is 3 and B is 5; A is .5 and B is 7.5; and on and on. She also knows that there are many incorrect solutions, such as A is 5 and B is 4, and so forth. She knows enough about the rules of arithmetic to distinguish between a correct and an incorrect solution. But she is bothered that there are so many correct solutions and wonders which one of the correct solution is the best one. However, she is not given any criterion to use to make this decision. Therefore, this is a partially specified problem.

2. Incomplete process linking beginning point with solution
   - One or more steps that would be needed to arrive at one "right" solution in the problem-solving process are missing.
   - **Example:** Carrie is preparing for her midterm exam. She has spent 20 hours reading the 10 assigned chapters in the textbook, and she has made detailed notes from the 20 hours of classroom lectures she attended. That totals 40 hours worth of input, yet the exam is only one hour long. How can she put herself in a position to write for one hour and show her professor she has absorbed 40 hours' worth of knowledge? She needs help in muddling through this process from a clear beginning point (her set of notes) to a clear end point (writing a correct and complete answer from her knowledge).

     Maybe the professor will ask exam questions that sample from the 20 classes; in that case, he might ask about material from only five classes. But the professor has not specified which lectures to focus on. Instead, Carrie would have to accesses the relative importance of the lectures on her own to decide which to study hardest.

     Or perhaps the professor will ask questions that will require her to look for a pattern across all lectures, then synthesize her opinion from this pattern. How can she do that? The professor never told the class what his informed opinion was, so Carrie cannot memorize the professor's sanctioned opinion. Instead Carrie would have to think for herself and decide which elements in the lectures and reading are relevant for the formation of her own opinion and assemble those elements into a well reasoned opinion she could present as her own.

An education composed of *only* learning the solutions to fully specified problems, however, is not a very useful one, because most of the problems people encounter in life are not fully specified. In a good college education, most of the problems we confront are partially defined and can *never* be fully specified. These are problems such as:

- Would psychoanalysis be an effective treatment for Internet addiction?
- Is *Great Expectations* or *David Copperfield* the better novel?
- Why did the principle of "economy of scale" work against X company and lead to its bankruptcy?
- Should the U. S. Constitution be amended to change the process of how a bill becomes a law? If so, how?

These are much more interesting questions than the fully specified ones, because they ask you to think much more deeply about the nature of things—such as the treatment of mental illness, the quality of literature, the limits of business principles, and the nature of government. These questions also allow you more freedom to look at things from different perspectives, to form your own opinions, to engage your own emotions, and to "peel the onion" layer by layer to gain deeper insights. In short, these partially specified problems can help you learn more about the topic—as well as about yourself.

Partially specified problems do not exist solely in college courses. They are everywhere. We encounter them all the time in our everyday lives, such as:

- Should I ask X out on a date?
- Why don't I like the music of Britney Spears anymore?
- Should I stay home and study tonight or go for a long run?
- Why don't I have more friends?
- Am I in love?

Students willingly struggle with the solutions to these problems, knowing that they are part of everyday life. However, when they face this type of problem in a course, they may back off from the challenge, waiting for a professor or a textbook to give the one and only correct solution. Exercise 1.1 offer an opportunity to practice recognizing types of problems.

EXERCISE 1.1

PRACTICE RECOGNIZING TYPES OF PROBLEMS

Which of the following are examples of fully specified problems and which are partially specified problems?

1. $(2 + 6 + X) / 3 = 5$

2. $(6 + 4 + X) / 2 = 3X$

3. $2 + X + Y = 10$

4. City X and City Y are 200 miles apart and linked by a train track. Train Number One leaves the station in City X at noon heading toward City Y. At the same time, Train Number Two leaves City Y traveling toward City X. Both trains travel at the same speed. At what mile marker will the trains pass each other?

5. Train Number One leaves the station in City X at noon heading toward City Y, which is 1,000 miles away. Train Number Two leaves City Y at 1:00 p.m. traveling toward City X. Both trains travel at 70 miles per hour. At what mile marker will the trains pass each other?

6. A red train leaves the station in City X at noon heading toward City Z at 60 miles per hour. At the same time a blue train leaves City Z traveling at 80 miles per hour. City X and City Z are 560 miles apart. At what mile marker will the trains pass each other?

7. In a vote by a legislature, a bill gets 55 votes. Does it pass and become a law?

8. Joey is a 12-year-old boy who has just watched half an hour of World Wrestling Federation. His younger sister comes into the TV room, grabs the remote control, and changes the channel. Will Joey act aggressively toward her?

9. When will the U. S. economy get better?

Answers

1. This is a fully specified problem. There is one unknown, X. The solution is 7.

2. This also is a fully specified problem. Although X shows up twice in the equation, X is only one unknown. The answer is 2.

3. This is a partially specified problem, because there are two unknowns and only one equation.

4. This is a fully specified word problem. Because the trains travel at the same speed and leave at the same time, they should be expected to pass each other at the halfway point—at the 100-mile marker.

5. Although a bit more complex than the previous word problem, this too is a fully specified word problem. Because the trains travel at the same speed, they should be expected to meet halfway—at the 500-mile marker. However, Train One leaves an hour early, so when Train Two leaves City Y, Train One is 70 miles from City X. They will meet halfway between those points, or 535 miles from City X.

6. At first glance, this might appear to be a fully specified problem. However, when you look more closely at the problem, you will notice that there is no information about where the blue train is headed. That is a crucial piece of information that is not provided. You could transform this into a fully specified problem by learning that the blue train is indeed heading toward City X.

7. This is a partially specified problem, because it is missing two pieces of information. First, we are not told how many members are in the legislature and if the bill needs a majority, a plurality, or a certain percentage of the vote to pass. Second, we are not told if there are steps beyond the vote in order for the bill to become a law. Perhaps a member of the executive branch of the government needs to sign the bill; perhaps a general election

is required. However, you could make this into a fully specified problem by finding out more about the rules for a bill becoming a law.

8. This is a partially specified problem. It is tempting to jump to the conclusion that Joey will scream at his sister and grab the remote control. However, we don't know enough to conclude this. Perhaps the sister has just come back from the doctor after getting her broken arm put in a cast after she was assaulted by the neighborhood bully. In this case, Joey would be feeling protective of his sister and would not get angry at her. Or perhaps Joey was responsible for his sister's broken arm and he is feeling remorseful. However, you could transform this into a more fully specified problem by finding out more information about Joey and his sister.

9. This is a classic partially specified problem. There are hundreds of factors that influence the economy. Also, there are many economists who continually track these factors and make predictions, and most of those economists are wrong at any given time. Still it is a fascinating and important problem, so people continue to address it. You can work to make it less partially specified by gathering information on the hundreds of factors over time and plotting trends. This will serve to reduce the ambiguity in the problem, but it will not take you all the way to a solution in which you can have 100 percent confidence.

Types of Partially Specified Problems

Partially specified problems come in two flavors. In the first kind, there is *not one clearly best answer.* That is, several people could all solve the problem with different solutions. No solution is more correct than the others, so we are not sure which is THE solution. An example is Y + Z = 24.

Another example is the problem of where to go for dinner. There are many good restaurants, each with its own advantages and disadvantages (quality of food, service, atmosphere, price, distance from home, and parking). Considering the advantages and disadvantages of each restaurant is like comparing apples and oranges. Usually there are many solutions to this problem, but which one is the best? What this problem is missing is a clear statement of the criteria for choosing one solution over the rest. Perhaps restaurant A has the best food, restaurant B has the best service, restaurant C has the best atmosphere, and restaurant D has the best prices. Each is a good choice of where to eat dinner tonight, until you state the criterion that should be used. If you have little money, then price is the most important criterion, and restaurant D is the best solution. We find ourselves stuck with a partially specified problem when we haven't stated what a good outcome would be.

The second type of partially specified problem has *an incomplete process;* there are steps missing that are needed to arrive at the specific solution. Think of a professor giving you some information to begin a project (such as a term paper), providing some examples for what the outcome of the project should look like, but then not telling you the full set of steps you have to take to complete the task. Often, the professor *cannot* tell you all the possible steps required to gather information, evaluate it, arrange it, and write it up, so you must figure it out for yourself. You might be given some overall guidelines, but those guidelines will be too general to cover every situation. When you run out of guidelines, you must continue on your own (perhaps asking friends or family for advice).

Another example of partially specified problems is what happens in detective stories. There is a clear ending point (solving the crime), but the process of arriving at this discovery is always different, because the facts of each case are different. In each story, the detectives have to construct their own process as they move toward solving the crime. They may stumble because they are missing important clues or don't know which information is important. Of course, the detectives stick with it until they gather the facts they need and assemble them into a solution.

Partially specified problems are not uncommon. People often encounter them in everyday life. With most of these everyday partially specified problems, we quickly craft a solution and then move on. The consequences of being wrong are usually trivial. However, when people must make a decision that has major consequences, they may agonize over the solution. Knowing that there is no one right answer and that there's no recipe for the solution, we might ask other people what they would do. If we find that most people would do the same thing, we often follow their advice. However, if they offer a variety of suggestions, we must make some assumptions and engage our feelings. We use those to help us, knowing that we are "making it up as we go along."

For example, think back to how you went about choosing a college to attend. There are 2,400 bachelor's degree–granting institutions in this country. How did you reduce this set of options down to a single choice? You probably had some stated criteria, such as limits on cost, geographical boundaries, or limits on colleges you thought might accept you as a student. However, even with these constraints, you were still likely to have had dozens of choices. You might have decided on some other specifications on your own, such as size of school and majors offered. This would have narrowed the choices down further. At this point, you might have chosen a number of schools and sent applications to them all. Perhaps you were accepted by more than one, and your problem was not solved until you chose one.

Choosing a college is a partially specified problem, and the fact that you are taking this course means you solved this very important and complex problem. It might have been partially defined by specifications that were given to you before you started, and you may have added some specifications as you narrowed down your choices. However, you still had to move beyond the specifications in order to arrive at a solution—and you did. The point is that you have already encountered lots of partially specified problems and solved them—even some very important ones. You are not new to this. The task for you is not learning how to solve partially specified problems; instead, the task is learning how to solve partially specified problems *efficiently and with a high degree of confidence.*

Strategic Thinking Points

- Our society is saturated with information, and that saturation is growing at an accelerating rate.
- The flood of information presents all of us with two fundamental challenges: *filtering* information and *using* the information we attend to.
- These two fundamental challenges are composed of partially specified problems, that is, problems for which we do not have a full set of guidelines to solve. In real life, we seldom encounter a problem that is fully specified. Therefore, it is essential to learn how to solve partially specified problems.
- In some educational experiences, we face fully specified problems and are expected to learn the set of steps to solve them. This approach works in lower grades and in college introductory courses where we learn the simple problems.
- The purpose of *higher* education is to practice confronting and solving more difficult problems. When you are able to recognize what is missing in partially specified problems and to use the information you have to span the gaps in those problems, you develop more professional skills and, the most practical of all, real-life skills.
- When you learn how to become a strategic thinker, you will be better able to meet the challenges of higher education efficiently and effectively. You will also be better able to meet the challenges of living in our information-saturated society.

CHAPTER 2

Strategic Thinking

LEARNING OBJECTIVES

By reading this chapter, you will:

1. Develop an understanding of the purpose of knowledge structures and how they serve both a mapping and an organizing function.
2. Learn that there are eight skills that are the primary tools of strategic thinkers.
3. Learn that the problem-solving process requires the use of algorithms and heuristics.

*B*ecoming a Strategic Thinker will help you meet the challenges of filtering and using information to solve problems in our message-saturated society. Recall that strategic thinking is an active and optimistic approach to learning. Strategic thinkers are aware of challenges and eagerly encounter them, because they are excited by the challenges and confident in their abilities not just to meet the challenges but to excel.

This chapter will show you how strategic thinking can help you meet the challenges presented in the previous chapter. First, you will learn why knowledge structures are important, then you will be introduced to the eight skills that are the key tools for the strategic thinker. With this information as a foundation, you will be better able to navigate through the problem-solving process.

KNOWLEDGE STRUCTURES

*S*trategic thinkers are able to make good decisions about which information to seek and how to use that information to solve problems. They are good at these decisions, because they can "see the big picture" and thus know what to look for. This big picture resides in a person's mind in the form of a set of **knowledge structures.** Think of knowledge structures as pictures of organized information.

Knowledge structure
The organization of information; exists in a person's mind, constructed by the person.

Knowledge structures serve two functions. First, they provide the *map* of a topic. When you have a map, you know how things fit together. You know where you are and where you want to go; this guides you in your search for information. When you start a course, you draw from what you already know to get oriented and get a sense of what to expect. If it is about something brand-new to you, you enter the course with a small knowledge structure containing only a few bits of information. If you work hard in the course and learn a lot about the topic, you finish with a larger, more elaborate knowledge structure that organizes the many pieces of information you picked up during the course. Such a knowledge structure serves as a map for all subsequent courses and experiences on the topic.

A second function of knowledge structures is to guide you in *organizing* new information. With a well-developed knowledge structure on a topic, you can easily make sense of new information as you encounter new messages on that topic. A knowledge structure helps you quickly *catalog* new information. This makes the new information easy to retrieve later when you need to use it.

To understand the cataloging function of knowledge structures, think about how people arrange the objects in their bedrooms. Some people's rooms look like a hurricane has blown through. Clothes, books, posters, hobby items, empty wrappers of food, and all sorts of other things are scattered randomly around the room. In contrast, other people have their things arranged in a neat, orderly fashion: Clothes are all folded or hung up and sorted by type. Books are aligned neatly on shelves. Things like empty candy wrappers and pizza boxes that are no longer needed are thrown out. Both kinds of people might have the same objects brought into their rooms, but the first kind of person has simply acquired a lot of items—and all appear to have equal importance. The second type of person has been making conscious decisions about what to throw out and how to arrange those things that are kept. This type of person knows where everything is and can quickly find anything. In contrast, the first type of person doesn't know how to find things, so he often gives up looking before finding what he knows is somewhere in the room. In frustration he goes out and gets new things, uses them, then throws those onto the growing pile of unsorted objects, and the clutter gets worse.

Why bother to make the effort to organize? The answer is: to achieve efficiency. Of course, if time is not important and you have all day to look for a piece of paper in your room, then the clutter is not a problem. However, most people feel they don't have enough time to do all the important things they want to do, so they have a high need to be more efficient—that is, do more in less time. The key to achieving efficiency is to get organized and to do a little bit of work each day to stay organized, so that when you need something, you can find it quickly.

Knowledge structures change as we deal with information. When we add new information, the knowledge structure becomes more elaborate and detailed. This elaboration makes the knowledge structure even more useful to us. If the new information reveals that old information in our existing knowledge structure is out of date, we cut out the old and insert the new.

What Is a Strategic Thinker?

- Strategic thinkers prefer knowledge over information.
  - Information is piecemeal and transitory.
  - Information resides in the messages, while knowledge resides in a person's mind.
  - Information gives something to a person to interpret, while knowledge reflects that which the person has already interpreted.
  - Knowledge is structured and organized, and it has enduring significance.
- Strategic thinkers rarely find value in simply memorizing facts, because they know that when they have memorized a list of facts, they have not created knowledge; all they have done is acquired a pile of "info-bricks" and have not built anything with those materials.
- Strategic thinkers know that they must construct knowledge structures for themselves, so they must actively do something with the information they encounter. No one can give them these structures, and they cannot memorize them. They need to construct knowledge structures piece by piece so that those structures become the very context of how they think.
- Strategic thinkers are careful in determining the value of information, so they have few inaccurate facts in their knowledge structures.
- Strategic thinkers are well organized; they know how to process new information very quickly and catalog it in the proper place, so they can find it when they need to retrieve it.
- All of us have knowledge structures, whether we are strategic thinkers or not. The difference is that strategic thinkers have better knowledge structures and more of them.

All of us have knowledge structures, whether we are strategic thinkers or not. For example, you have a knowledge structure about music. When you hear a piece of music, you instantly know where it belongs in your music knowledge structure. That is, you know the rules about types of music well enough to be able to identify a particular song as being rock, rap, country, classical, jazz, polka, or something else. Think of the knowledge structure as a tree with branches. You may have major branches for rock, rap, blues, and country/western. Your rock branch might have its own branches: head banger, metal, hard rock, soft rock, and golden oldies. Your knowledge structure is different from my knowledge structure for music, because we have each constructed our own structure from our own experiences. Your knowledge structure may have many sub-branches (and even sub-sub branches) for rap because you have spent a lot of time listening to that type of music. This would mean you can see big differences among rap artists. In contrast, I may have only one branch for rap music, so I catalog all rap artists in that one branch; I don't know enough to see the differences between various rap artists. However, I have many sub-branches for jazz and make many distinctions among jazz artists.

The fact that our knowledge structures are different does not mean mine is better or worse than yours. What makes one knowledge structure better than another is when it is broader. Being broader means it can guide us in a wider range of experiences. The fact that my music knowledge structure is missing a lot of detail in the area of rap limits my ability to appreciate that art form. It is not possible for me to make good evaluations about who are bad rap performers, who are good, and who are great. I am missing a part of life, because I am limited in my appreciation for this type of music. Thus, knowledge structures that are broad, with many branches, each with a good amount of detail, are much more useful, because they can guide people in many different experiences.

All messages—whether they come from the media, people, or any other source—arrive with the assumption that you have the context needed to understand their meaning. That context is in your knowledge structures. Thus, knowledge structures are an essential tool for understanding the meaning of any message, and the more highly developed your knowledge structure is on a topic, the more quickly and accurately you can understand the meaning of a message.

SKILLS

K nowledge structures must be constructed. The raw materials we use to construct them are bits of information. The tools we use to construct them are **skills.**

Skills

Abilities that people use as tools to process information and create knowledge structures.

We live in an information-saturated society, so getting access to the raw materials is not much of a problem. Therefore, the key to becoming a strategic thinker is in developing strong skills. People who have weak skills will not be able to do much with the information they encounter. They will ignore much of the good information and will focus on information that is often inaccurate or useless. They will organize information poorly, thus creating weak and faulty knowledge structures. In the worst case, people with weak skills will try to avoid thinking about information altogether and become passive. When this happens, the active information providers—such as advertisers and entertainers—will become the constructors of people's knowledge structures and will take over control of how these people see the world.

You are probably already very familiar with one skill: memorization. This is the ability to retain facts by cataloging them in your memory in a way that lets you access them later. This is an important skill, but there is much more to acquiring a good higher education than merely retaining facts. Your mind is not merely a recording device for other people's messages—it can do much more. If you learned only by absorbing messages intact and unaltered, you would have far less knowledge than you actually do. Where does all this other (nonmemorized) knowledge come from? You construct it yourself, and if you are able to construct it well, you will excel in your college courses—especially those beyond the introductory levels—and you will get much more out of life itself.

In order to construct knowledge well, you need to develop what I call the "eight skills of higher education." These eight skills build from memorization and give you the ability to take the facts you memorize and transform them into something new. This process of absorbing new information and elaborating your knowledge structures to accommodate it is what creates understanding.

What are these eight skills? They are *analysis* and *evaluation,* which help you filter information; *induction, deduction, grouping,* and *synthesis,* which help you construct understanding; and *abstraction* and *persuasive expression,* which help you share knowledge (see the box below). While some of these terms may appear

The Eight Skills of Higher Education

Filtering Messages

1. **Analysis**—searching for particular elements in messages; requires breaking down a message into meaningful elements
2. **Evaluation**—judging the value of an element by comparing the element to some criterion

Constructing Understanding

3. **Grouping**—determining which elements are alike in some way and which elements are different in some way
4. **Deduction**—using general principles to explain particular elements
5. **Induction**—inferring general patterns from the observation of particular elements
6. **Synthesis**—reassembling elements into a new structure

Sharing Knowledge

7. **Abstracting**—stating a brief, clear, and accurate description of a message
8. **Persuasive expression**—expressing knowledge in a clear and compelling way in order to convince the reader of the value of that knowledge

strange or new, they refer to skills you use all the time in everyday life, whether you know their names or not. Chapters 4 through 11 will guide you to strengthen your existing skills and help you avoid traps that can prevent you from using your skills well.

Filtering Messages

The first task when you encounter a message is filtering. Filtering does not mean ignoring. Ignoring is unconscious, while filtering is conscious; you make a decision to screen in or screen out a message. If you ignore the message, there is no filtering. If you attend to a message, then there is filtering, which results in the message being consciously screened out (rejected) or screened in (considered for incorporation into your knowledge structures).

This filtering task relies on two skills—analysis and evaluation. *Analysis* means searching for something in the message. Sometimes the message will contain many elements, but you may be interested in only one element. You break the message down into its component parts in order to select only the one part you want. Other times, you may want to understand the composition of the entire message, so you break it down into components in order to see what those components are and how they fit together. The product of the analysis is a set of elements, which then become the raw material to be used by the skill of evaluation.

Evaluation is the skill used to assess the worth of the elements by comparing them to some standard. Those elements that are found to have little or no value for some purpose are filtered out. Those that are judged to have high value are filtered in. These valued elements then become the raw material of the tasks in the next stage.

Constructing Understanding

A prevalent problem with the information we encounter is not just that there is so much, but also that it frequently appears random and fragmented. Sometimes it seems to be an endless flow of facts, where each fact is disconnected and totally unrelated to the facts preceding and succeeding it. What does it all mean? In some courses, professors will interpret the information for you and *tell* you what it means. More often than not, however, especially in more advanced courses, professors present the information and ask you to construct your own meaning. Knowing how to construct meaning well is the hallmark of an educated person.

We must do something with the information we filter into our consciousness. What we do is construct meaning, and to do this we use four skills: grouping, induction, deduction, and synthesis. These four skills are tools we can use to work with the new information and fit it into our existing knowledge structure on a topic. As we add this new information, the knowledge structure is changed. If new information shows that old information is incorrect, the new information replaces the inaccurate information. New information that fills in a gap makes the knowledge structure more complete. New information that confirms existing information gives the knowledge structure greater detail and weight. Thus by incorporating new information, we can correct problems with the previous knowledge structure or make it grow in breadth (new topics) or depth (additional elements on an existing topic in the structure).

The *grouping* skill lets you decide where new information should be cataloged in your existing knowledge structure. To do this, you compare and contrast. When new information is similar to a particular set of information already in the knowledge structure, you catalog it there. When the new information is different from the information in the existing knowledge structure, you use it to form a new branch or to replace an existing branch (if the old information is faulty).

The skill of *induction* lets you find patterns. When you add new information, it might fill in gaps so that now you can see connections among other elements. Once you see a pattern, you can generalize it to explain all possible elements in the set. For example, imagine when you meet your roommate you find out he is on the football team. You meet the person across the hall and find out he is on the swim team. Then you meet someone from down the hall and find out she is on the basketball team. You see a pattern: all are athletes. Even though you have only met three of the maybe 100 people in your dorm, you conclude that you are living in the athletic dorm. You have generalized a conclusion beyond the pattern you found among the three people, and you are applying your conclusion to everyone in your dorm.

The *deductive* skill is useful when you are not sure where a new element should be placed. In the process of deduction, you use general principles to come to a conclusion about a specific person or thing. For example, let's say over time you have developed the general principle that in order for professors to be good teachers, they need to be friendly to students. You notice that Professor Jones is friendly to you and other students. Therefore, using deduction, you conclude that Professor Jones is a good teacher.

The skill of *synthesis* lets you arrange a new element along with other elements from different parts of your knowledge structure to construct a new configuration. This new configuration is not merely the addition of an element to an existing part or the addition of yet one more example to an already perceived pattern. Instead, synthesis results in a wholly new branch in a knowledge structure. It relies on the other skills, but it is more ambitious in its goal and more creative in its execution. For example, if you take apart your car, then put it back together so it works, that is not synthesis; that is re-assembly. However, if you take apart three cars that do not work well, throw out the parts that are broken, then put the good parts together as a new car that works better than any of the original three cars, that is synthesis.

Sharing Knowledge

Sharing knowledge is an important stage of learning. Although sharing knowledge usually benefits other people, the primary benefit is to the person who is sharing. The act of sharing knowledge forces you to clarify meaning for yourself. When you share knowledge, you are able to check that the meanings you constructed in your own thought processes make sense to other people. This is why people often say they learn more when they have to teach something to others than when they simply try to learn it for themselves. Sharing knowledge uses the skills of abstraction and persuasive expression.

To be successful with these skills, you need a good knowledge structure to work from, but if your knowledge structure needs work, practicing these skills can also help you improve it. A well-communicated message is a strong indication of a good knowledge structure, and it also serves as an opportunity to improve your knowledge structure. As you apply the skills of abstracting and persuasive expression, you may see ways to change your knowledge structures for the better.

The skill of *abstracting* is used when we want to relay the essence of some message to another person or to record the essence of that message in some way so we can refer back to it later. When the message to be abstracted is complex or new and there is no obvious formula to follow, the task can be quite challenging.

Abstracting is something you already do. People often abstract in an informal way, for example, when they tell someone what a movie was about. They try to capture the essence of the entire movie in a few minutes of words.

The skill of *persuasive expression* may at first seem to be too limited. Why not deal with a skill of expression in general? My answer is that—to varying degrees—all expression is persuasive. When you are trying to get other people to change their opinions about something, obviously you are being persuasive. However, you are also being persuasive when you are presenting what *appears* to be purely descriptive information. The truth is, no message is purely descriptive. For example, if your girlfriend asks you what you did last night while she was studying, she does not want a simple description of your schedule. It will not satisfy her if you say, "I met some friends for dinner at the Brown Pelican at 6:00. Then we drove to the cineplex and saw a movie until 9:00. Then we drove back to the dorm and hung out until midnight then went to bed." From what you know about your girlfriend (your knowledge structure about her), you might know that she wants to be persuaded that you could not possibly have a good time without her. So you would say something like, "I was lonely without you, so I found a few people to have dinner with me at the Brown Pelican, because I know you don't like that restaurant. We couldn't think of anything better to do, so we went to a movie then we went back to the dorm. We talked, mainly about you, until about midnight and I went to bed." Both stories contain the same facts, but the second one would have much more meaning to your girlfriend, because it persuades her that you missed her rather than simply describing how you spent the time. Because the first story lacks that element, it might seem to her that you are trying to hide something, and she may be persuaded that you don't really think much of her or that you are closer to your other friends. These are not what you intended to convey, but you left it up to her to fill in the gaps, and she has persuaded herself of things you do not want her to believe. Persuasion still occurred, but it was she and not you who did the persuading. In order to be a more effective communicator, you need to be aware of your goals, then craft messages that will achieve your goals rather than let other factors govern the persuasion.

All messages are your interpretations of events and people. When you tell people about things, you are in essence telling them that your interpretation has value and that they should consider it useful to them.

Although the eight skills were presented above in three groups (filtering messages, constructing understanding, and sharing knowledge), the skills can be used in any order. They can also be used in any combination.

Now that you have learned more about what it means to be a strategic thinker, consider Exercise 2.1. Which of the two women is more of a strategic thinker?

EXERCISE 2.1

WHO IS THE STRATEGIC THINKER?

Consider the following two scenarios and pick out the strategic thinker.

1. As Audrey drives to the airport, she passes hundreds of signs and billboards along the road. She has her car radio on but is not paying attention to the songs or ads, although she finds the songs soothing. When the songs are interrupted for an ad, she pushes a button and changes the station. When the weather report comes on, she turns the volume up and listens carefully. When she gets near the airport she begins paying attention to signs so that she can find long-term parking, her check-in counter, and her gate. While she waits for her plane to board, she scans through discarded newspapers to pass the time, but nothing triggers her attention. She goes to the newsstand and browses through the magazines, again just killing time. An announcement that her plane is boarding grabs her attention. Once on the plane, she puts on headphones and listens to the airplane music while she tries to fall asleep.

2. As Belinda is driving to the airport, she passes many billboards but does not pay attention to them until she gets near the terminal, then carefully looks for signs to direct her to parking, her check-in counter, and her gate. In the car she is listening to a tape that she checked out from the library. The tape gives information on the topic of the presentation she has to make in her destination city. At the airport, she scans the magazine racks to find articles relevant to her topic. She buys three magazines, then reads only those articles relevant to her topic, ignoring the rest of the information. On the plane, she reads through two books on her topic—moving very quickly through information that she already knows and slowing down to critique and absorb the new information. Throughout the day, her selection of information is conscious, and she is guided by a plan. Whenever she encounters new information, she carefully scans it for messages to answer particular questions.

Can you spot the strategic thinker? The difference is not what happens to the person; both are exposed to many messages. Neither is the difference that one pays attention to all messages while the other pays attention to none of the messages. As you likely noticed, both attend to some and ignore others.

For the answer, see the box titled "Answers to Exercises" at the end of this chapter.

THE PROBLEM-SOLVING PROCESS

As a strategic thinker, you are well equipped to handle partially specified problems as well as fully specified problems. You realize that you must take a different approach to the problem-solving process when the problem is only partially specified.

Problem-solving process
The path that starts with the posing of a problem and moves through gathering information and reasoning toward the solution.

Problem solving is a process. It begins with an awareness of a challenge you face. You search your mind for information relevant to the challenge. If you find enough information, it is likely that you have a fully specified problem and that you can readily arrive at a solution by following what is called an *algorithm*. However, if you do not have enough information to arrive at a solution, you must search for more information. Even when you have gathered a great deal of information, there are times when you still cannot solve the problem, because you are not sure what to do with the information. That is, the formula you are using to solve the problem has some missing parts. In this situation, you need more than an algorithm; you also need some *heuristics*. You may not have heard the terms "algorithms" and "heuristics" before, but they will become part of your everyday vocabulary as you develop into a strategic thinker.

Algorithms

Algorithm
Set of rules that prescribes how to solve a problem in a step-by-step, logical manner.

For some types of problems, people have developed standard rules that lead to a solution. These are called algorithms. An **algorithm** might be a formula or a list of steps. It tells you what to do step by step. If the problem is fully specified, then the algorithm will tell you all you need to know in order to solve the problem with confidence. If followed accurately, an algorithm guarantees that in a finite number of steps you will find a solution to the problem.

Even with partially specified problems, algorithms still help, but these algorithms rarely take you all the way to a solution. They leave out parts of the solution path. How do we bridge over these gaps along the problem-solving path? Systematic, logical reasoning cannot help you across the gaps (if it could, it would be part of the algorithm).

When algorithms reach their limit of usefulness, human judgment comes into play. This is usually the place where computers stop having value in solving problems. Computers can move down the path to this point much faster than humans, but then they freeze up when they run out of rules. What do humans do to press on? They employ what cognitive psychologists call *heuristics*.

Heuristics

Heuristics
Suggestions about how to work through gaps in the problem-solving process.

Heuristics are suggestions about how we should go about exercising judgment. They are guidelines or recommendations more than rules. While algorithms are specific rules for moving logically to a problem's solution, heuristics are suggestions of ways to proceed to a solution under conditions of uncertainty. Heuristics *can* lead you to solutions. However, there is no guarantee that heuristics will get you all the way to a solution, or that, if they do, the solution will be a good one.

In order for heuristics to work well, we need to regard the heuristic as only a suggestion—a suggestion that requires us to use techniques such as lateral thinking, metaphor, personal judgment, and even intuition. When we use these techniques well, we can arrive at good solutions to partially specified problems. However, when we do not use these techniques well, we can fall into all kinds of traps that prevent us from arriving at a good solution or even at any solution at all.

Lateral thinking. Most people are taught to solve problems by thinking sequentially—beginning at the first step and continuing one step at a time all the way to the one solution at the end of the path. This "vertical" form of thinking is concerned with achieving a solution by using a logical process. It is efficient when it keeps us on track toward a goal and prevents us from wandering into unproductive or incorrect thought processes.

We can, however, arrive at faulty conclusions when we use **vertical thinking.** Sometimes vertical thinking sets us off down a faulty path, and even though we are very logical in proceeding down that path, we still end up with the wrong conclusion. For an example, try Exercise 2.2. Did you see the error in thinking? Now try some lateral thinking challenges in Exercise 2.3, and see if you can find solutions to these problems by thinking "nonvertically."

Vertical thinking
Solving a problem with logic by moving systematically step by step to a solution.

EXERCISE 2.2

STUCK IN VERTICAL THINKING?

The Scenario

An interviewer is looking at two applications he was just handed by two women applying for the same job. He notices that the two women have the same last name. Also, they share the same address and the same telephone number. The name of their mother is the same on both applications. The name of their father is the same on both applications. They were born in the same town on the same date—same month, same day, and same year.

The interviewer looks up at them and notices that they look remarkably alike. He says, "You two must be twins."

They smile back at him and say, "No."

How is this possible?

Most people would reason from the evidence and arrive at the same conclusion: The two women are twins. The reasoning process is as follows:

> There are two women.
> They share the same last name (possibly a coincidence).
> They share the same address (again maybe a coincidence).
> They share the same mother (they must be at least half sisters).
> They share the same father (they must be full sisters).
> They share the same birth place and birthday.

Conclusion: They *must* be twins because they were born in the same place, at the same time, and from the same parents.

The reasoning from the evidence is very systematic and shows no errors in logic. Why is the conclusion wrong?

For the answer, see the box titled "Answers to Exercises" at the end of this chapter.

EXERCISE 2.3

LATERAL THINKING PUZZLES

1. Look at the following sequence of letters: M T W T. What should be the next letter in the sequence?

2. A cabin, locked from the inside, is perched on the side of a mountain. It is forced open, and 30 people are found dead inside. They had plenty of food and water. They were not poisoned, and there were no suicide notes. There are no weapons inside. How can you explain this?

3. Consider the following word: **boas.** Can you re-arrange the letters in that word to arrive at another word that refers to something you use to keep you clean?

4. Mr. and Mrs. Jones were young and active people. Their next-door neighbor, Mrs. Jackson, was a 93-year-old invalid. One day, the Jones asked Mrs. Jackson into their house to do something neither one of the Jones could do. There was no skill that she had that they didn't have, so why did they need Mrs. Jackson?

5. A man was driving his car at high speed when the car spun off the road, crashed through a fence, and bounded down a steep ravine into a fast-flowing river. As the car settled in the river, the man realized he had broken his arm and could not release the seatbelt and get out of his car. The car sank to the bottom of the river with him trapped inside. He was found alive by rescuers who arrived two hours later. How is this possible?

6. A man rides into town on Friday. He stays three nights and leaves on Friday. How is this possible?

7. Three castaways were starving on a desert island. When they had run out of food, they decided that one of them had to die to be eaten by the other two. All three were single and were of the same age, experience, size, and skills. But they easily decided who should die. How?

8. A man had some wood. On Monday, it was the shape of a cube. On Tuesday, he changed it into the shape of a cylinder, and on Wednesday, he changed it into the shape of a pyramid. He did not cut or carve the wood into these shapes. How did he do it?

9. A truck became wedged under a low bridge. It could not move forward or backward without severely damaging its roof. The truck driver was perplexed until a little girl standing nearby suggested an easy solution. What was it?

10. A man pushing his car stopped outside a hotel. As soon as he got there, he knew he was bankrupt. Why?

11. A man had a jug full of lemonade and a jug full of milk. He poured them both into one large vat, but he kept the lemonade separate from the milk. How?

12. A helicopter was hovering 200 feet above the sea. The pilot turned the engines off, and the rotors stopped. Yet the helicopter did not crash. How?

For the answer see the box titled "Answers to Exercises" at the end of this chapter.

Sometimes you will be moving smoothly down the problem-solving path—systematically following a step-by-step procedure, as specified in an algorithm—but then you will suddenly run into a barrier, unable to move to the next step in the algorithm. When you cannot move straight ahead, you need to move laterally to get around the barrier: You need to do some lateral thinking. **Lateral thinking** means brainstorming possible alternative paths around the barrier.

Lateral thinking is a way of restructuring old patterns to gain new insights. It is not meant to generate the one "right" answer; instead, it is helpful in suggesting new approaches. Therefore, lateral thinking is most useful when we are stuck in a partially specified problem, and logic does not help us move toward a solution. One way to think laterally is to think in terms of metaphors.

Lateral thinking
Brainstorming to envision alternative paths to a solution.

Metaphors.   The essence of a **metaphor** is its evocative power to help us understand one thing in terms of another. Often when we encounter something new, in order to see its nature, we liken it to something with which we are already familiar.

When you are trying to solve a problem and run into a barrier, you can use metaphors to think about alternatives to giving up. For example, let's use the game of football as a metaphor for a partially specified problem. If you can't run the ball straight ahead (i.e., think vertically toward a solution), then you need to run around the end; once you turn the corner, you can see some daylight and run for the end zone (solve the problem). Or you could throw a long pass (jump over the barrier). By looking for connections between strategy in the game of football and strategy in the process of problem solving, we can use football to give us a new perspective on our present situation. This fresh perspective might suggest some creative ways to attack the problem at hand or at least help us break out of where we are stuck.

Sometimes, the metaphor we try turns out to be inappropriate, and it is difficult to perceive connections between the metaphor we chose and the problem we are trying to solve. For example, if you are trying to decide which college to attend and you choose yogurt as a metaphor, you are not likely to get anywhere. You want a college that comes in a small container, tastes good, and is not past its expiration date? No, that will not work as a metaphor! How about college as a dry cleaner? (You want a college that will make you look great, not shrink you, and not cost too much?) Dry cleaner is a little better as a metaphor for colleges than is yogurt, but you can probably think of many metaphors that are even better.

Playing with metaphors keeps your thinking fresh by helping you perceive things from different perspectives. One of these perspectives might suggest an innovative solution path. Try Exercise 2.4 to get an idea of how metaphors can help you solve problems.

Metaphor
A figure of speech that illustrates the characteristics of something by suggesting a resemblance to something else.

EXERCISE 2.4

PLAYING WITH METAPHORS

1. Let's say you are trying to impress a potential romantic partner, but this person regards you as a rat. "Rat" is an animal metaphor that does not suggest good characteristics for a romantic partner.
   - Think about what positive characteristics you would most like to be perceived as having.
   - Can you think of an animal that has those characteristics?

- What other positive characteristics does that animal have?
- Now, what animal metaphor should your romantic partner use instead of rat?

2. Think of your life as a song. Which well-known song would it be?
   - What type of music is it? (rap, rock, classical, country, blues, jazz, etc.)
   - What emotions do the lyrics portray? (silly, serious, sad, angry, sexy, etc.)
   - Is the song fast or slow?
   - Is the song more background music or in-your-face music?
   - Is the song an old traditional standard or a brand-new cutting-edge song?
   - Are many instruments or few instruments playing the music?
   - Now think about all the characteristics about the song you can (use the list above to get started). Then look at the pattern of those characteristics. What do they say about what you think of your life?

3. Think about your college career as a car. What kind of a car would it be?
   - Would it be a fuel-efficient compact or a huge SUV?
   - Would it be sporty and racy or safe and practical?
   - What kind of fuel would it take and how many miles to the gallon?
   - How much maintenance would it require and how much would it cost to insure it?
   - Would it have room for lots of people and things, or would it be a small two-seater with quicker, easier handling?
   - Now think of all the characteristics of the car you selected as a metaphor for your college career. What does it say about how you perceive college—that is, how much you put into it and what you expect to get out of it?

Did any of the metaphors above help you see yourself with a fresh perspective? Keep playing with metaphors. Think of yourself as a breakfast cereal, a resort, a sport, a color, a period of history, a type of math, a store, and more. Be creative!

Some educators even regard metaphors as the key to knowledge, because all new knowledge is first encountered in terms of experience with existing knowledge. Again, this is why having good knowledge structures is so important. When you encounter new information, you search your existing knowledge structures for something that looks and acts like the new information. Something that "looks or acts like something else" is a metaphor. Metaphors, then, give us the insight to understand something new in terms of our understanding of something old and familiar.

Personal judgment.   Some tasks are usually presented in the form of fully specified problems. For example, a spelling problem is usually solved by recalling information that you memorized before. If I asked you to spell the word "chair," you can do it without having to exercise any judgment. However, if I asked you to spell a word that you had not memorized, you would not have so much confidence. Instead, you might feel like you had to make a wild guess. However, often a *wild* guess isn't necessary; instead you can use good **personal**

Personal judgment
Inferring conclusions based on one's own experience.

judgment to make an *educated* guess. You can use what you know about translating sounds into letters, the spelling of other English words, and other guides (such as "i before e except after c") to construct a reasonable spelling. It requires judgment to translate rules that were designed for one kind of a problem to try to solve a different kind of problem.

Intuition.   The use of heuristics often benefits from a dose of intuition. By engaging the emotions, **intuition** helps us guess what could be plausible solutions without having to go through a systematic process. Often the insightful guess or the creative leap to a tentative conclusion can help us see a reasonable solution that we could not see by reason alone.

> **Intuition**
> Spontaneous insights that do not arise from logical reasoning.

Exploring hunches can be useful. However, we should not rely solely on hunches or intuition to solve problems, especially important ones. Intuition is one of many useful tools—but not the only tool of an educated person.

CONCLUSION

You probably have heard the phrase "Once you understand the problem, you are already halfway to a solution." This saying is true in the sense that the more clearly you understand a problem, the easier it is to move toward a solution. It also helps to know the type of problem—that is, whether the problem is fully specified or partially specified. If the problem is fully specified, then it provides enough information for you to solve it. When this is the case, the process of solving it is relatively simple. However, if the problem is not fully specified—which is the case with many problems we encounter in our everyday lives—the construction of a good solution is much more challenging and requires a different approach.

The problem-solving process can be guided by algorithms. When the problem is fully specified, we only need to learn the correct algorithm and then apply it. However, most problems are only partially specified, so the problem-solving process has gaps, and the guidance provided by algorithms alone is incomplete.

How do we span the gaps? We need heuristics. Whereas algorithms are rules, heuristics are suggestions. Algorithms give us the steps of how to apply our skills in solving a problem. Heuristics tell us what to think about when we encounter gaps in that process. This serves to help us shift our perspective, see the problem in a new way, construct elements to help us bridge the gaps, then eventually complete the problem-solving process. A good problem solver must be able to apply both algorithms and heuristics. The stronger your skills, the better you will be able to use both.

If you are to be successful in solving partially specified problems, you cannot be stopped by the gaps where you don't have enough information. Instead, you need to use the information you have to construct the additional information you need, then use that newly constructed information to bridge over the gaps and keep progressing toward a solution. Heuristics can help you construct those missing pieces by providing guidelines that tell you what to think about as you build the bridges over the gaps.

Does this mean that this process of solving challenging problems is idiosyncratic? Yes—each challenging problem is different in what it leaves unspecified. Thus, no one can provide you with a set of rules—an algorithm—that lays out a complete set of steps to solve any partially specified problem. Instead, algorithms only provide rules for general processes; they give you only a generic structure that helps you get started solving different kinds of problems. You will also need to use heuristics. Heuristics are less formal, less constraining, less directive than algorithms. They give you freedom to try different things in different sequences.

The heuristics we use are influenced by context (our knowledge structures). Because different people have different knowledge structures, they use slightly different heuristics and thereby end up with different solutions. Heuristics rely more on lateral thinking than vertical thinking. They nudge us to be more creative by suggesting metaphors. They privilege individual human judgment and intuition, rather than relegating these characteristics to second-class status in problem solving.

Answers to Exercises

FOR EXERCISE 2.1: WHO IS THE STRATEGIC THINKER?

The key difference is in how the two women encounter information and what they do with it. With few exceptions (such as the weather report), Audrey is not monitoring her environment well. She does not have an agenda for information, so there is nothing for her to seek out actively. In contrast, Belinda carries around some important questions in her mind and is constantly scanning the environment for information that would help her answer those questions. At the end of the day, Audrey will have the same knowledge structures; she has gotten through the experience by making her plane flight successfully but has little else to show by way of accomplishments. Belinda ends the day with knowledge structures that are more detailed and elaborated. She has absorbed more information from her environment, but not just any information. She has absorbed the bits of information she could use and incorporated them into her knowledge structures. Belinda has actively analyzed messages, evaluated elements in those messages, and brought elements into her existing knowledge structures by using her skills of grouping, induction, deduction, and synthesis. When she was planning her presentation, she was working on her skills of abstraction and persuasive expression.

On the surface, both women spent the day in a mundane task of traveling. However, one woman made the most of her time and by the end of the day had even stronger skills and more useful knowledge structures. The more these two women spend their time in the ways described, the wider the gap between them will grow. Belinda is on a trajectory to become more successful in her job, more in control of the information in her environment, and more knowledgeable about life.

FOR EXERCISE 2.2: STUCK IN VERTICAL THINKING?

The conclusion is wrong because the two women are not twins; they are two sisters in a trio of triplets.

What went wrong in the reasoning process is that the interviewer fixated on the two people. As he began noticing similarities among the two, he tentatively concluded they were twins. This tentative conclusion was strengthened as he observed each additional similarity until he was absolutely convinced of his conclusion. He was very systematic and logical in his thinking after he jumped to the wrong conclusion, and this systematic reasoning kept him on the same path he originally set out on, even though it led to the wrong conclusion. By reasoning vertically, he stayed focused on a single path, and this logical path created blinders that prevented him from seeing other alternative conclusions. The blinders were set at the very beginning and he was unable to think beyond "two."

He needed to break out of vertical thinking to consider that these two sisters might have other sisters who were also born at the same time. Because he stayed with vertical thinking, he kept going over the steps in his systematic thinking to find his error. But there was no error in his systematic thinking; the error was in his faulty beginning assumption that there were only two sisters.

FOR EXERCISE 2.3: LATERAL THINKING PUZZLES

1. The next letter should be F. The letters in the sequence are the initials standing for the days of the week.
2. It was an airplane cabin from a plane that crashed into the mountain.
3. The answer is "soap." The b in boas had to be rotated to appear as a p.
4. Mrs. Jackson was needed to witness the signing of a legal document.
5. The river was shallow, and the water came up only to the man's chest.
6. Friday is a horse.
7. One of the three people was a strict vegetarian. He agreed that he should naturally be the sacrifice.
8. The wood was in the form of sawdust.
9. The girl told the driver to let some air out of his tires.
10. The man was playing a game of Monopoly.
11. The jugs were full of frozen cubes of lemonade and milk.
12. The helicopter landed on a helipad on an oil platform at sea.

CHAPTER

3

Knowledge Styles

LEARNING OBJECTIVES

By reading this chapter, you will:

1. Learn that your knowledge style is composed of your cognitive abilities and emotional abilities as they relate to encountering information.
   - Cognitive abilities include: field independence, crystalline and fluid intelligence, vertical and lateral thinking, and conceptual differentiation.
   - Emotional abilities include: emotional intelligence, tolerance for ambiguity, and non-impulsiveness.
2. Learn about three types of knowledge styles: Information avoider, consumer, and strategic learner. By taking a diagnostic test, you will identify your own knowledge style and learn what this means to you.
3. Learn how knowledge styles are shaped by four factors: innate abilities, maturation, conditioning, and self-improvement through active practice.

Knowledge style
A person's approach to encountering messages and transforming information into knowledge.

Each of us has an individual knowledge style. Your **knowledge style** is your perspective on approaching information, that is, how you go about perceiving, processing, and organizing it. In short, it is your basic approach to the task of constructing knowledge structures.

Many different kinds of knowledge styles exist, but this chapter focuses on three. By taking the Knowledge Styles Diagnostic Inventory, you'll find out which of the three is most like your style.

The more you know about your knowledge style, the more clearly you can understand your strengths and weaknesses. This information will help you develop your skills to higher levels. Please take the Knowledge Styles Diagnostic Inventory in Exercise 3.1 now, before you read any further. Think about what you like and don't like in general about education and the courses you have taken. Then respond to the 30 items honestly. When you have finished scoring this diagnostic test, go on to page 36 and continue reading the chapter.

EXERCISE 3.1

KNOWLEDGE STYLES DIAGNOSTIC INVENTORY

For each of the 30 items below, decide whether the description fits you, then write the appropriate number from the following scale next to the item.

0 = Not at all like me
1 = A bit like me
2 = Like me
3 = Very much like me

_____ 1. When I encounter a new idea in a course, I like to analyze it in depth.

_____ 2. The most important element in any course is a well-prepared teacher who can present the information clearly.

_____ 3. I don't like memorizing lots of material.

_____ 4. I like courses where we deal with a few topics but really analyze them in depth rather than courses where we cover many different topics but don't go into much depth on any one.

_____ 5. I dislike tests where you're supposed to guess what the teacher wants.

_____ 6. In many courses, I just can't get started.

_____ 7. While the teacher is lecturing, I often find myself thinking beyond the points he or she is trying to make.

_____ 8. It is important for teachers to hand out study guides before the test so I can know what I should study.

_____ 9. When I have a difficult problem, I like to "cut to the chase" and make a quick decision rather than doing a lot of work that might not amount to anything.

_____10. Not all ideas in a course are equally important; I like to decide for myself what is important more than I want my teacher to make that decision for me.

_____11. During class, I try to write down everything the teacher says.

_____12. My teachers usually lecture in a way that is hard to follow.

_____13. I get excited by challenges; the harder the challenge, the more excited I get.

_____14. I do not like the teacher to waste class time by getting off the track by telling irrelevant stories that won't be on the tests. Teachers should stick to the facts.

_____15. If I do not understand the course material, I try not to worry about it.

_____16. When I run into something that does not immediately make sense, I keep working with it and analyzing it until I really understand it.

_____17. I think test questions should be taken directly from the class notes. It's not fair when the teacher surprises me with a test question over material we did not cover in class.

_____18. I prefer that the teacher never call on me during class.

_____19. The learning challenge I like the most is the task of trying to make order out of chaos.

_____20. My confidence level in a course is highest when the course has a lot of well-organized facts that I can memorize easily.

_____21. It is the teacher's job to motivate me to do my best work.

_____22. I'm the kind of person who likes to set my own goals for learning, even if they are very different from the teacher's goals in the course.

_____23. When I am exposed to new information, I want my teacher to tell me what is most important.

_____24. No matter how hard I work, I never seem to do as well as I would like.

_____25. When my teachers give a reading assignment, I like it when they don't tell me what to look for in the reading; I like to determine what is important for myself.

_____26. I hate courses where the instructor gives you lots of readings and you have to figure out what is important in those readings.

_____27. If I don't learn much in a course, it is usually because the material was too hard.

_____28. I am often frustrated in courses when we don't examine something in enough depth to find out what is really going on.

_____29. During the first class meeting, I want to get an accurate idea of how hard the course will be.

_____30. When I get a low grade on a test or an assignment, I feel frustrated and it is hard to shake that feeling.

When you have finished storing all 30 items, go to Exercise 3.3 at the end of this chapter to tabulate your results and find out what kind of knowledge style you have.

COMPONENTS OF KNOWLEDGE STYLES

A person's knowledge style is composed of both cognitive and emotional components. The cognitive component refers to the way we *think*, while the emotional component refers to how we *feel* about information. Those feelings can motivate us to search out and analyze information—or they can prevent us from working with information. The cognitive and emotional components interact to form a person's knowledge style.

In the following sections, I will present four cognitive abilities and three emotional abilities that together make up your overall knowledge style. You have developed these abilities over years of being in school. Students who have fewer of these abilities have to work harder to get the same rewards as other students who have more of these abilities. Thus, in order to become an even more successful and efficient learner, you will need to develop as many of these abilities as you can.

Cognitive Abilities

Some people can memorize facts very well; others cannot. Some are able to think about problems in many different ways; others seem stuck in one perspective when they view a problem. Some people continually play with information by creating new categories and looking for patterns; other people either try to ignore information or try to find quick and easy ways to deal with it. Knowledge styles are characterized primarily by four cognitive abilities: *field independence, crystalline and fluid intelligence, vertical and lateral thinking,* and *conceptual differentiation.*

Field dependency.   Perhaps the most important characteristic in your cognitive style is field dependency. Think of field dependency as your natural ability to distinguish between the "signal" and the "noise" in any message. Noise is the chaos of symbols and images. Signal is the information that emerges from the chaos. People who are highly field dependent get stuck in the field of chaos—seeing all the details but missing the patterns and the "big picture," which is the signal. **Field-independent** people are able to sort quickly through the field to identify the important elements and ignore the distracting elements.

Field independence

Ability to see the big picture by perceiving important information in the mass of details.

For example, when they are watching a story during a television news show, field-independent people will be able to identify the key information—the who, what, when, where, and why of the story. They will quickly sort through what is said, the graphics, and the visuals to focus on the essence of the event being covered. People who are field dependent will perceive the same key elements in the story but will also pay an equal amount of attention to the background elements: how the news anchors are dressed, their hairstyles, their makeup, the color of the graphics, and so forth. To the field-dependent person, all of these elements are of fairly equal importance, so the person is as likely to remember the trivial as to remember the main points of the story. This is not to say that field-dependent people retain more information, because they pay attention to more. To the contrary, field-dependent people retain *less* information, because the information is not organized well and is likely to contain as much noise (peripheral and tangential elements) as signal (elements about the main idea).

Here's another example. Have you ever had to read a long novel and gotten so lost about 100 pages into it that you had to quit in frustration? You may have felt that just when the author was getting the story going with one set of characters, she would switch to a different setting at a different time with a totally new set of characters. This may have been happening every few pages! There were too many characters talking about too many different things. You were overwhelmed by all the detail and could not make sense of the overall story. When this happened, the novelist was making demands on you to be much more field independent than you could be. If you had been more field independent, you would have been able to see through all the details and recognize a thematic pattern of some sort, then use that thematic pattern as a tool to sort through all the details (characters, settings, time, dialog, and action) in order to direct your attention efficiently to those elements that were most important.

Field dependency is not a categorical thing. It is not that some people are purely field dependent while others are purely field independent. There is a range of field dependency, and people vary by degrees. To estimate your position on the continuum, try the simple test in Exercise 3.2.

EXERCISE 3.2

DIAGNOSING FIELD DEPENDENCY

The Exercise

1. Close this book.

2. On a piece of paper, jot down the main idea in this chapter plus three subsidiary ideas that amplify that main idea.

Diagnosis

This might seem like an unfair exercise. After all, we are only about one quarter of the way through the chapter and I'm asking you to articulate the major idea of the chapter! However, that is the point of the exercise—to find out if you are focusing on the big picture or if you are plodding through the chapter sentence by sentence.

If you were able to do this exercise with no negative emotion and with confidence in your answers, you are relatively field independent. You are reading actively and continually asking yourself "What is most important?" Before reading this chapter, you probably looked carefully at this chapter's outline at the beginning of the book, then you scanned through the chapter to get a feel for its structure of main points. With this structure in mind, you were able to navigate your way efficiently through the reading so far, adding detail to your structure at appropriate places. So when I asked you to close the book and write down the main idea, you already had a picture of the entire chapter and were able to do this exercise easily.

If instead you struggled with this exercise, you are less field independent, because you did not have the "big picture" of this chapter clearly in your mind. As you were reading, you were probably giving each sentence and each idea equal weight. So when I asked you to write down the most important ideas, you probably listed the most *recent* ideas you encountered. Or perhaps you were able to list 10 or 12 points but not able to decide which of those were the most important. Or perhaps you could not list any points at all—in which case the experience of reading was probably an unrewarding struggle for you. You forced your eyes over each line of type, but your mind was not distinguishing the ideas (signal) from the lines of type (noise).

Field-independent strategies require a little more work up front when you are beginning to read a chapter. However, this investment of effort at the beginning will pay big dividends, making it possible for you to read much more efficiently and with much more confidence.

We live in a culture that is saturated with information. Much of it is noise. The sheer bulk of all the information makes it imperative that we sort the important from the trivial. However, many of us are overwhelmed by all the information and do not bother to sort. Instead we default to a passive state as we float along in this stream of messages. Developing one's cognitive style requires taking a more active role and consciously sorting. The ability of field independence makes the sorting easier and more rewarding.

Crystalline intelligence
Ability to think systematically and memorize facts.

Fluid intelligence
Ability to think creatively and construct nonformulaic solutions to problems.

Crystalline and fluid intelligence. It is helpful to think of there being two types of intelligence: crystalline and fluid. **Crystalline intelligence** is the ability to memorize facts. Highly developed crystalline intelligence allows a person to absorb the images, definitions, opinions, and agendas of others.

The other type of intelligence is fluid; this is the ability to be creative and see patterns in complex sets of facts. Highly developed **fluid intelligence** gives us the facility to challenge what is on the surface, to look deeper and broader, and to recognize new patterns.

Both types of intelligence are important for strategic thinking. People with strong crystalline intelligence can absorb and retain basic information, such as definitions, lists, dates, names, and other elements that can be memorized. People with strong fluid intelligence can creatively bridge the gaps of information in partially specified problems. When the two types of intelligences work together, they form a much more powerful knowledge style. The creative thinking of fluid intelligence works better from a strong base of information provided by crystalline intelligence.

Vertical and lateral thinking. Most people are vertical thinkers (recall that this idea was introduced in Chapter 2). Vertical thinking is systematic, logical thinking that proceeds step by step in an orderly progression. A student needs this type of thinking to learn the introductory information on any topic. We need to be systematic in order to learn basic arithmetic, spelling, and dates in history.

Lateral thinking, in contrast, does not proceed step by step. Instead, when confronted with a problem, the lateral thinker jumps to a new position that might seem random and unconnected, then works backward and tries to construct a logical path between this new position and the starting point. Lateral thinkers are more intuitive and creative. They reject the standard beginning points to solving problems and instead begin with an intuitive guess, brainstorming, or a proposed solution "out of the blue." The lateral thinker works backward from innovative conclusions to the beginning of a problem. A lateral thinker tends to arrive at solutions that other thinkers would never imagine, because they are locked into a rigid form of thinking.

Few people have a natural aptitude for lateral thinking. Those who do have such aptitude use it often. Inventors and scientists usually produce a string of new ideas, not just one. For example, Thomas Edison invented so many things that by the end of his life he had more than 1,300 patents in the areas of the telegraph, telephone, phonograph, movie camera, and projectors. This suggests that there is a human capacity for generating new ideas that is better developed in some people than in others. This capacity does not seem to be related to sheer intelligence but more to a particular way of thinking. There are smart and not-so-smart lateral thinkers, just as there are smart and not-so-smart vertical thinkers.

Both forms of thinking have advantages and disadvantages. Vertical thinkers perform well at solving traditional problems for which algorithms exist. However, when their traditional methods of solving problems break down and they reach a dead end, they are stuck and have nowhere to go. When this happens, often it is the lateral thinker who breaks through the barrier. On the other hand, lateral thinkers can often be "flighty"—they may come up with many unique ideas, none of which actually work or are feasible ways of solving a problem. People who are good at both kinds of thinking and who know when to try each approach are, of course, the most successful problem solvers.

It is easier to teach vertical thinking than lateral thinking, because vertical thinking is a process of systematically following steps and procedures. In contrast, lateral thinkers approach things from a different and creative point of view, which is difficult to teach. Because it is easier to teach and evaluate the quality of vertical thinking, educational institutions focus much more on vertical thinking at the introductory level, where you need to absorb the formulas and lists that authorities deem most important. However, once you get beyond this type of learning, you will encounter more significant challenges where you will need to solve partially specified problems. You will need to move beyond memorizing information and instead look for fresh patterns, synthesize your own opinions, and project future trends. These more challenging tasks will frequently present barriers that can be circumvented only through lateral thinking.

Conceptual differentiation. The degree to which people group and classify things is called **conceptual differentiation.** People who classify objects into a large number of mutually exclusive categories exhibit high conceptual differentiation. In contrast, people who use a small number of categories have low conceptual differentiation.

Related to the number of conceptual categories is category width. People who have few categories usually have broad categories so as to contain all types of messages. For example, if a person only has three categories for all media messages (e.g., news, ads, and entertainment), then each of these categories must contain a wide variety of messages. In contrast, someone who has a great many categories would divide media messages into thinner slices (e.g., breaking news, feature news,

Conceptual differentiation
Ability to break things into component parts and see finer and finer differences among things.

documentary, commercial ads, public service announcements, action/adventure shows, sitcoms, game shows, talk shows, cartoons, and reality shows).

Emotional Abilities

Your knowledge style is composed of more than cognitive abilities. It is also composed of emotional abilities that work together with the cognitive abilities. Some people are naturally excited by new information and have a strong drive to seek out more. Others feel exhausted when they encounter a new message, because they already feel overwhelmed by the flood of information in our culture. Three characteristics of emotional ability contribute to your knowledge style. These are: *emotional intelligence, tolerance for ambiguity,* and *non-impulsiveness.*

Emotional intelligence
Ability to recognize the emotions in ourselves and others, along with the ability to control emotions.

Emotional intelligence.   Our ability to understand and control our emotions is called **emotional intelligence.** Emotional intelligence is thought to be composed of several related abilities, such as the ability to read the emotions of other people (empathy) the ability to be aware of one's own emotions, the ability to harness and manage one's own emotions productively, and the ability to handle the emotional demands of relationships.

People with stronger emotional intelligence have a well-developed sense of empathy; they are able to see the world from another person's perspective. The more perspectives people can access, the more emotional intelligence they have. People who are highly developed emotionally are more aware of their own emotions. They also better understand the factors that cause those emotions, so they are able to choose messages that get the emotional reactions they want. In addition, they are less impulsive and are able to exercise more self-control. They can concentrate on the task at hand rather than becoming distracted by peripheral emotions.

Tolerance for ambiguity
Ability to keep working on unclear problems until they are solved.

Tolerance for ambiguity.   Every day you encounter people and situations that are unfamiliar to you. To prepare yourself for such situations, you have developed sets of expectations. What do you do when your expectations are not met and you are surprised? That depends on your level of **tolerance for ambiguity.** If you have a low tolerance for ambiguity, you will likely choose to ignore those messages that do not meet your expectations; you might feel too confused or frustrated to work out the discrepancies.

In contrast, if you are willing to follow situations into unfamiliar territory that go beyond your preconceptions, then you have a high tolerance for ambiguity. Initial confusion does not stop you. Instead this confusion might motivate you to search harder for clarity. You do not feel an emotional barrier that prevents you from examining messages more closely. You are willing to break any message down into its components and make comparisons and evaluations in a quest to understand the nature of the message and to find out why your initial expectations were wrong.

Non-impulsiveness
Ability to slow down and reflect on problems rather than quickly jumping to conclusions that are often false.

Non-impulsiveness.   People's ability to control their emotions when dealing with information is called **non-impulsiveness.** Some people get swept away with negative emotions, such as frustration or anger. They cannot control their emotions, so they let those emotions force them to make quick decisions so as to eliminate the negative drive. When people make decisions too quickly, their choices are usually not optimal.

Decision-making typically involves a trade-off between speed and accuracy. A person who is impulsive makes decisions very quickly in order to move out of the uncomfortable emotions. However, people who take time to reflect usually make better decisions. Those who take a long time and make few errors are *reflective,* and those who are quick and make many errors are *impulsive.*

How much time a person takes to make decisions is governed by his emotions. If he feels comfortable encountering new information and likes to work through problems carefully, he is likely to act reflectively and take his time. However, if he feels a negative emotion (such as frustration), he will tend to make decisions as quickly as possible in order to eliminate the negative emotional state.

TYPES OF KNOWLEDGE STYLES

W hen we consider the four cognitive abilities and the three emotional abilities together in all possible combinations, we can conceive of many different types of knowledge styles. Rather than inventory all those possible knowledge styles here, let's focus on three that are likely to be the most prevalent. These three knowledge styles are: information avoiders, consumers, and strategic learners. While most people have a bit of all three, one of these styles is usually dominant.

Information avoiders do not avoid *all* information, but they do avoid a much higher percentage than people with other knowledge styles. These people typically feel so overwhelmed by information that they keep their minds on autopilot almost all the time. They ignore almost all information unless something breaks through their consciousness and requires their attention. However, because these people have few interests (other than protecting themselves from new ideas), seldom does a message break through their consciousness and capture their attention.

Information avoider
A type of knowledge style; information skills are weak and there is resistance to working with new facts.

Information avoiders are not without opinions, but those opinions typically have been given to them by other people. These people usually don't want to go to the trouble of constructing opinions for themselves. They feel more comfortable accepting the opinions of other people than working at developing their own. Then, once they accept an opinion, they don't want to be challenged, so they avoid almost all information. The information they do pay attention to is typically information that confirms what they already know. This makes for a more comfortable existence; however, this also greatly limits their knowledge about the world.

Information avoiders have weak information-processing skills, which makes it difficult for them to deal with much information. To avoid this difficulty, they try to ignore challenging information and filter in only confirming information. Confirming information requires very little mental processing. Challenging information demands that we process it—to evaluate its credibility, to find more information on the topic, to synthesize the new information into our existing knowledge structure. Information avoiders do not like this challenge. By filtering in only information on topics that they feel they already know a good deal about, these people reduce their risk of being challenged and thereby protect themselves from potentially negative emotions.

This is the least desirable knowledge style. Because information avoiders are so risk averse, they do not get much out of their encounters with information. They close themselves off more and more from the world, preferring instead to live inside their own minds, where their existing beliefs get stronger and stronger while outside information becomes more and more irrelevant.

If you have all—or many—of the characteristics listed in the box below, it is likely that your primary knowledge style is the information avoider. The more of

Profile of the Information Avoider Knowledge Style

- *Field dependence.* Information avoiders have a lot of trouble discerning what is important in messages, so they miss the point of many messages and therefore would rather avoid them altogether.

- *Weak fluid intelligence.* Information avoiders do not like the challenge of solving problems, preferring to let things work themselves out on their own. Also, they do not like trying to think of things in new ways. An information avoider makes a decision quickly and resists reconsidering it, avoiding change.

- *Weak crystalline intelligence.* Information avoiders find it difficult to memorize things, so they use lots of mnemonics to keep things in their short-term memory long enough to do well on tests of memorization.

- *Weak vertical and lateral thinking.* Information avoiders resist the work required to reason systematically. While they may appear intuitive in their opinions and even wild in their generalizations, they do not do what good lateral thinkers do, which is to carefully check their intuitively constructed guesses against the facts in order to determine if those guesses are valid or useful.

- *Weak conceptual differentiation.* Information avoiders tend to have few categories for information. Rather than working to acknowledge differences and create new categories, their attitude toward new information that does not fit into existing categories is either to ignore the information or simply throw the new information into the easiest category and justify it by saying, "Whatever!"

- *Low emotional intelligence.* When information avoiders feel negative emotions as they encounter information, they are not sure how to deal with these emotions other than to retreat. Thus, negative emotions form a barrier between them and the information.

- *Low tolerance for ambiguity.* Information avoiders are quick to avoid messages that introduce uncertainty or complexity. Over time they narrow their exposure down to fewer messages so that they always stay with what is familiar and thereby protect themselves from having to expend more mental effort.

- *High impulsiveness.* Information avoiders dislike uncertainty, so they make decisions as fast as they can. They feel that sacrificing accuracy is a small price to pay for escaping the negative emotions that characterize decision-making situations.

these characteristics you have, the more difficult it will be for you to develop your skills of strategic thinking. Of course, you are not likely to be an extreme information avoider, or you would not be reading this book—or any book for that matter. If you are an information avoider, try to understand your knowledge style and how it is preventing you from doing better in school. With this self-awareness and a commitment to change, you can begin to alter the knowledge style you currently have.

The **consumer** knowledge style (see the box below) provides a stronger base for learning than the information avoider style. Consumers value information and

Consumer
A type of knowledge style; convenience and efficiency are valued; there is a desire for as many facts as possible but a resistance to spending effort.

Profile of the Consumer Knowledge Style

- *Field dependence.*   Consumers have a lot of trouble discerning what is most important in messages. They need someone else to tell them what is important; for example, before each test they tend to ask for a study guide so the professor will tell them what is important, rather than feeling confident figuring this out for themselves.

- *Strong crystalline intelligence.*   Consumers are successful at memorizing lots of facts. To consumers, facts, not skills, are the commodities to be acquired in the supermarket of education.

- *Weak fluid intelligence.*   Consumers do not have a great deal of educational experience or positive reinforcement in problem solving or creative thinking. They believe that truth rests in the expertise of authorities, such as teachers and texts. They have low confidence that something they construct (a conclusion, opinion, or solution to a problem) on their own will be valued.

- *Relatively strong vertical thinking.*   Consumers want to follow rules in order to move to a solution as efficiently as possible. They are skeptical of lateral thinking, because it is often not efficient in the short term. They are uncertain that any proposed solution will work. They prefer to have someone tell them the best solution method, then vertically follow that path.

- *Relatively strong conceptual differentiation.*   Consumers absorb other people's category schemes, even if those schemes are very complex and contain many categories and sub-categories, but they typically are not good at constructing them for themselves.

- *Relatively good emotional intelligence.*   Consumers tend to use their emotions well to focus on material while they try to memorize it.

- *Low tolerance for ambiguity.*   Consumers are quick to avoid messages that introduce uncertainty or complexity. Over time they narrow their exposure down to fewer messages and experiences so that they always stay with what is familiar and protect themselves from having to expend more mental effort.

- *Relatively good non-impulsiveness.*   Consumers want to achieve accuracy—but only up to a point. When the costs get too high, they switch to a criterion of efficiency, and this can lead to impulsive decisions. Consumers sometimes feel that sacrificing accuracy is a small price to pay for getting past the decision-making situation and on to other things.

actively seek it out. Consumers are also very good at memorization. When the information in a course consists mainly of facts—such as lists, names, dates, definitions, and formulas—consumers usually do well. However, they perform less well in courses where they must analyze material for themselves, make their own judgments about the value of information, see patterns underlying large numbers of facts, or synthesize solutions to partially specified problems.

The skill of memorization helps consumers acquire large numbers of facts, but that skill alone does not help them do something with the facts to transform them into meaningful knowledge. However, transforming facts is not a concern to consumers. Consumers do not see facts as raw materials to be used to build knowledge structures, but as prepackaged knowledge that is simply handed to them. Consumers regard education as a supermarket (see the box below) providing a wide variety of packaged facts.

Education as a Supermarket (A Metaphor)

People with the consumer knowledge style regard educational institutions primarily as supermarkets of facts. Being driven by the goals of efficiency and convenience, consumers expect the following experience of college, the "knowledge supermarket."

Consumers expect the knowledge supermarket to be well organized so they can navigate through it as quickly as possible. This means each product should be arranged in its own department—fresh produce, household cleaners, deli, bakery, and so forth. Consumers have a list of the facts they need, and they want to visit the sections of the store they like (physical sciences, social sciences, humanities, arts, etc.) and stay away from other sections of the store.

Consumers like the products on the shelves to be stacked neatly in well-labeled packages so they are easy to find. If facts are hard to find, consumers get frustrated quickly. They want to be able to find what they need, put it in their cart (memorize the fact), and get on with the rest of their shopping.

Consumers tend to like brands where there is no assembly required, that is, where facts have already been assembled into knowledge by the "manufacturer" (the professor). This provides the shopper greater convenience. To illustrate, consumers prefer to buy a cake at the bakery rather than a cake mix. If the bakery has no cakes, the consumer will then settle for a cake mix (if it requires little work) over buying all the individual ingredients (flour, sugar, butter, salt, etc.) and then having to make the cake themselves. They like to shop but not to cook.

Not all shoppers are consumers. Some shoppers prefer to buy fresh ingredients, then follow their own recipes. They like to cook and know how to do it well. They take satisfaction in improving their recipes and their cooking skills. For these shoppers, convenience is less important than nutrition or taste. Shopping is only the first step in food preparation.

The **strategic learner** is the strongest knowledge style. If this is your knowledge style, you are fortunate to have been born with many natural abilities that would make you a good student or to have developed them during your education (see the box below). Also, you are likely to have had good instruction that has challenged you over the years to help you hone your abilities.

Strategic learner
A knowledge style; many abilities (both cognitive and emotional) combine.

INFLUENCES ON KNOWLEDGE STYLES

K nowledge styles are influenced by the dynamic interaction among four factors: innate abilities, maturation of cognitive and emotional abilities, conditioning through experience, and self-improvement through active practice.

Profile of the Strategic Learner Knowledge Style

- *Field independence.* Strategic learners have the ability to focus on the essence of messages and keep other details in the background. When encountering information, they quickly and accurately distinguish the signal from the noise.

- *Strong crystalline intelligence.* Strategic learners have the ability to memorize lots of detail (short-term memory) as well as the ability to retain detail for long periods of time (long-term memory). Highly developed crystalline intelligence allows them to absorb the images, definitions, and opinions of others.

- *Strong fluid intelligence.* Strategic learners are able to find creative solutions to problems and innovative ways of organizing information. Highly developed fluid intelligence allows them to challenge what appears on the surface, to look deeper and broader, and to construct new patterns in areas where other people accept the old patterns.

- *Strong vertical and lateral thinking.* Strategic learners use both types of thinking. Most important, they know when to use one or the other.

- *Strong conceptual differentiation.* Strategic learners are willing and able to construct many categories for information so that the differences and similarities across messages are apparent. When they encounter information that does not fit well into their categorization system, they are willing to create new categories for that information.

- *High emotional intelligence.* Strategic learners have a great deal of understanding of their emotions, as well as the ability to control their emotions, especially in translating negative emotions into motivation toward goals.

- *High tolerance for ambiguity.* New and complex messages energize strategic learners. They are willing to meet the challenge of creating order out of chaos.

- *High non-impulsiveness.* Strategic learners refrain from jumping to conclusions too quickly merely to have decisions completed, because they prefer accuracy in decision-making over efficiency. They can be impulsive when efficiency warrants it, but their typical approach to information is to reflect on it.

Although the first two of these are largely outside of your control, you can exert some control over how your abilities are conditioned, and you can exert considerable control over their improvement.

Innate Abilities

Your knowledge style is how you approach information and what you do with it. People are not born with a knowledge style, but they are born with certain natural aptitudes that can shape the development of a knowledge style. Some people have higher IQs, some are naturally more field independent, and some seem to have been born with more developed creative abilities and a tendency to think laterally. Others have innate learning disabilities such as dyslexia that make it much harder for them to process information.

People also differ in their innate emotional abilities. Some are born with an emotional disability such as attention deficient disorder. Some have hair-trigger emotional reactions and are challenged to keep their emotions under control. In contrast, others were born with well-developed emotional abilities.

Innate abilities
Abilities that a person is born with.

Our **innate abilities** are given to us, but this does not mean that they are unchangeable. Many of these innate weaknesses can be overcome, either through maturation, conditioning, or self-improvement.

Maturation

Maturation
The process of acquiring more skills as a person's mind develops.

Innate abilities mature on their own early in our lives. This means that we get better at understanding concepts and in controlling emotions. Much of this **maturation** happens outside our control or awareness. Children find it difficult to comprehend certain ideas until their minds mature to a point. For example, you cannot teach a one-year-old child to add and subtract, no matter how good a teacher you are. The child cannot understand what adding and subtracting are and is not ready to learn them yet. Over the next few years, however, the child's mind matures and becomes ready to learn these things.

The leading thinker about human cognitive development, Jean Piaget, observed that a child's mind matures from birth to about 12 years of age; during this time it goes through several identifiable stages. Other psychologists have examined how the human mind matures beyond the age of 12. Psychologists still have a lot to learn about how humans develop cognitively and emotionally throughout the entire lifespan. However, what we do know is that we continue to mature on all sorts of abilities throughout both childhood and adulthood, and that patterns of maturation differ from person to person. We also know that there are some things we can do to accelerate certain kinds of maturation. There are other things we need to do to keep the process on track; if we neglect them, we may remain stuck at a low level of development for our entire adult lives.

Throughout the course of our lives, our natural abilities (or deficiencies) make it easier (or more difficult) for us to deal with the information we encounter. As we mature, our abilities improve. In addition to innate abilities and levels of maturation, another factor affects our knowledge style—perhaps more strongly than the two we've already discussed. That factor is conditioning.

Conditioning

Each experience you have with information conditions you. If an experience is pleasant, you will feel rewarded and will be more likely to seek that experience again. If you act on that motivation and seek out more information and that new experience is also rewarding, you will have an even stronger motivation to seek more of that information.

On this conditioning path, you will eventually encounter more difficult information—information that is either more complex, more ambiguous, or in conflict with what you think you already know. If you are sufficiently motivated, you will accept the challenge of making sense of this more difficult information. If you are successful, you will feel an even stronger reward.

The higher the challenge, the more you will feel rewarded when you are successful in encounters with information. The rewards condition you to keep on this path of encountering more and more challenging information. As you move along this path, your skills get better with practice, and when your skills are better, you can meet stronger challenges with even more significant rewards. This is the process of conditioning.

Conditioning can also move in a negative direction. If you have an unpleasant experience with some type of information, you will feel punished and be more likely to avoid that experience in the future. When you encounter information of this type again, you will be likely to ignore the information in order to avoid another unpleasant experience. Over time your avoidance of that type of information will be reinforced. You lose opportunities to develop a better knowledge structure on the topic. Also, you lose the opportunity to practice your skills, and they grow weaker. When skills are weaker, encounters with information are less rewarding, and emotional barriers may develop that wall you off from more information. The cycle is a downward spiral of emotions influencing cognitions, which in turn influence emotions.

Our knowledge styles are conditioned by our experiences as we interact with information and other people, especially in educational situations. For example, if you are average on cognitive intelligence, you will notice that there are other people around you who seem to learn faster and better than you do. These other people are labeled as the "smart kids" in school. If you are labeled as average or below average, you may be conditioned to have low expectations for your ability. These low expectations can lead you to work less and expect less from yourself. Eventually you will be conditioned to have low expectations for yourself. In this situation it can be very difficult to develop your skills. Conditioning has led you to a dead end where you now believe that you are limited and you cannot change. But perhaps the original diagnosis of your intelligence was faulty; perhaps you were of average or higher intelligence, but the person who criticized you did not see it. If this misdiagnosis set off a pattern of negative conditioning, that conditioning may have eroded your expectations until now you believe you are below average, and you act like it. Conditioning can erode your natural abilities, but it can also *increase* your abilities over time, if you stay motivated and work hard until the rewards start coming.

Another example of long-term conditioning is related to the emphasis in education on crystalline intelligence rather than fluid intelligence. Think back to the

Conditioning
Having one's approach to knowledge shaped by rewards and punishments. Rewards make an experience pleasant, and this conditions people to want to repeat the experience; punishments make an experience unpleasant, and this conditions people to want to avoid the experience in the future.

kinds of tests you have taken in high school and college. If you are like most students, you have taken many tests that measure your crystalline intelligence—that is, your ability to memorize lots of facts. You are not likely to have taken many tests that measure your fluid intelligence or your ability to be creative and think of novel solutions to problems. Therefore, you have had much more practice in using your crystalline intelligence and not much in using your fluid intelligence. Also, when you excel with crystalline intelligence, the rewards tend to be more visible than the rewards given for fluid intelligence. It is not surprising that in the general adult population, crystalline intelligence appears to be higher than fluid intelligence, and that crystalline intelligence continues to increase with age. Formal educational programs provide fewer opportunities to develop fluid intelligence than crystalline intelligence.

We are all conditioned by exposures to information. For some, that conditioning is in a positive direction, an upward spiral of rewards and skill improvement. Others are being conditioned in a negative direction, in a downward spiral of punishment, atrophying skills, and information avoidance. We cannot elude the conditioning process, but we *can* choose whether to follow the upward spiral leading to stronger skills and better knowledge structures or the downward spiral leading to avoidance and cognitive weakness.

Self-Improvement

All of us have the potential to continue developing our knowledge style at any point in life. Regardless of your innate abilities, you can still get better. Once you have reached college, you cannot rely on maturation for improvement; your mind has matured to a point where maturation is no longer a barrier—or a help. Regardless of how you have been conditioned, you can take control of your future. Even if you have been conditioned to believe you are not very smart, you can still improve. You can develop your skills on your own. To do so, you need to be committed to **self-improvement,** and you need to work on it.

Self-improvement
The process of developing stronger skills through guided practice.

CONCLUSION

The basis for all skills development is a person's knowledge style, which refers to how people perceive, process, and organize information. Knowledge styles are composed of cognitive and emotional components that work together. The three major types of knowledge styles include (1) information avoider knowledge style, characterized by weak skills that make encounters with information difficult, so these people choose to avoid as many of these unpleasant encounters as possible; (2) consumer knowledge style, characterized by seeking immediate efficiencies through the use of tactics that simplify tasks and provide structure by outside authorities; and (3) strategic learner knowledge style, characterized by a high attraction to all kinds of information and a strong set of skills to process that information.

Knowledge styles are influenced by a person's innate abilities, maturation, and conditioning. We are born with certain innate abilities and limitations; it is what we do with these abilities and how we allow the limitations to affect us over time that shape the development of our knowledge styles. Our cognitive and emotional abilities mature up to a point as we grow older. Conditioning also shapes our knowledge style. When we are rewarded in our encounters with information, we are conditioned to seek more information. When we are punished in our encounters with information, we tend to avoid future encounters. Conditioning usually comes from sources outside the individual (teachers, parents, friends, etc.) but we can also condition ourselves by how we reward or punish ourselves.

We can overcome the weaknesses in our knowledge styles if we first understand what those weaknesses are and have clear goals for what we want our knowledge styles to be.

EXERCISE 3.3

TABULATING YOUR RESPONSES ON THE KNOWLEDGE STYLES DIAGNOSTIC INVENTORY

Transfer the numbers you wrote on your questionnaire to the tabulation sheet below. Then sum the numbers down each of the three columns and write the totals at the bottom of the columns.

1. _____	2. _____	3. _____
4. _____	5. _____	6. _____
7. _____	8. _____	9. _____
10. _____	11. _____	12. _____
13. _____	14. _____	15. _____
16. _____	17. _____	18. _____
19. _____	20. _____	21. _____
22. _____	23. _____	24. _____
25. _____	26. _____	27. _____
28. _____	29. _____	30. _____
TOTAL _____	TOTAL _____	TOTAL _____

Circle the largest number of the three totals. If that circled number is more than 25 and the other two totals are below 15 each, then the circled number indicates your dominant style. If no total is more than 20 and especially if all three totals are similar (within about 7 points of each other), then you likely do not have a dominant style—that is, you have a mix of all three.

The right-hand column contains items that indicate an *information avoider* style. If your number in this column is large relative to the numbers in the other two columns, then you are likely to be an information avoider.

The middle column contains items that indicate a *consumer* style. If your number in this column is large relative to the numbers in the other two columns, then you are likely to think like a consumer.

The left-hand column contains items that indicate a *strategic learner* style. If your number in this column is large relative to the numbers in the other two columns, then you are lucky to have been born with many natural abilities that can make you a good student.

CHAPTER 4

Skill 1: Analysis

LEARNING OBJECTIVES

By reading this chapter, you will:

1. Learn how to conduct component analyses.
2. Learn how to conduct outline analyses.
3. Learn how to conduct focal plane analyses.
4. Understand how to use four types of heuristics to help you with the skill of analysis:

   - Purpose-defining
   - Inductively derived positions on dimensions
   - Identifying number of elements
   - Identifying number of levels

5. Understand how to avoid some traps that can prevent you from using the skill of analysis well.

The most fundamental of the eight skills of strategic thinking is the skill of analyzing. Analysis is the most basic skill, because each of the other seven skills requires the product of an analysis as their raw material.

Analysis is the skill used to sift through messages to identify their parts, to identify their structure, or to locate a fact. With the skill of analysis, we work with messages and try to identify particular elements in the message. Sometimes the elements are on the surface of the message and are therefore easy to find. Other times, the elements we are searching for are difficult to find. In this case, analysis is like looking for gold. A prospector searching for gold sifts through dirt to find the nuggets of gold, dips a pan into a running stream, and uses the pan as a sieve to catch the bits of gold (filtering in) while letting the water and debris run past (filtering out). Whether digging or panning, we know what we want, and we know we must search through a lot of material to find those valuable bits.

Individuals who are more field independent have an easier time using the skill of analysis; they can more quickly spot the gold nuggets. People who are highly field independent are good at clearly distinguishing between signal (what they are searching for) and noise (everything else) in messages. They can make fast and accurate decisions about what is important and what is background. However, with practice even people who are highly field dependent can learn how to do analysis well and become more field independent.

There are three types of analyses: component analysis, outline analysis, and focal plane analysis. All three require you to break the message down and look for something that exists within the message. Component analysis focuses on breaking down the message into meaningful parts. Outline analysis focuses on identifying how the elements in the message fit together. Focal plane analysis involves reading through the message to find an answer to a particular factual question.

COMPONENT ANALYSIS

Component analysis
Breaking a message into a set of components that are mutually exclusive and exhaustive.

The algorithm for conducting a **component analysis** has three steps. First, you must determine the purpose for your analysis. Second, you select the most appropriate dimension(s) to fulfill your purpose. Third, you use the dimension(s) to identify the full set of mutually exclusive elements. These steps form the component analysis algorithm.

Step 1: Determine Purpose

Any message can be analyzed for different purposes. For example, let's take something simple like a one-page, handwritten letter. If you are a detective, you might analyze the letter to identify its physical properties (such as the type of paper or the type of ink). A detective might also analyze the letter to identify the author through the handwriting, in which case the analysis would ignore paper and ink and instead focus on other components. If you are a teacher, you could analyze the letter to check that all the formal parts are there. If you are the recipient

---

The Process of Component Analysis

1. Determine your purpose for the analysis.
2. Select the most appropriate dimension(s) to fulfill your purpose.
3. Use the dimension(s) to direct your attention and look for the full (exhaustive) set of mutually exclusive elements on that dimension.

---

of the letter, you could analyze it for ideas or emotions. Even though this letter is a simple example, many purposes to guide a component analysis are possible.

Typically, you know the purpose for the analysis before you start, or you would not have been motivated to conduct the analysis. The key in this first step is to make sure you are clear about your purpose before you proceed.

Step 2: Select the Dimension(s) for Analysis that Will Fulfill Your Purpose

Once you are clear about your purpose, you need to select a dimension to use in conducting your analysis. Let's return to our example of the handwritten letter. A detective analyzing the letter to identify the author could use the handwriting as the dimension of analysis and break the letter down into units of handwriting (how the t's are crossed and the i's dotted) for later comparison against the handwriting of various suspects. A teacher analyzing the letter to check that all the formal parts of the letter are present would use the dimension of formal features and break the letter down into the date, address of recipient, salutation, body, and signature.

Sometimes the purpose for an analysis and the components to look for will be assigned to you. For example, a math teacher might ask you to read a chapter in a geometry book and identify all the theorems presented there. Or a literature professor might ask you to analyze a short story and identify the points of conflict. These are examples of more fully specified problems. However, if a literature professor asks you to read a short story and does not tell you what components to search for, you must decide this for yourself. How do you do this? The answer is that you need to use your knowledge structure about short stories to find the dimensions along which short stories can be analyzed. If you have a well-developed knowledge structure about short stories, then you will know that short stories can be analyzed along the dimension of character (find the main characters, the secondary characters, and so forth), plot (what is the generating circumstance, the points of heightening conflict, the climax of action, and the denouement), theme (what are the implications of characters' decisions and what does the action teach the reader), and emotion (which emotions are evoked in the reader by characters and their actions). People who have no knowledge structure about short stories will have no awareness of the options for analyzing them, thus this partially specified analysis problem will frustrate them. They are stuck, and they will stay stuck until either someone tells them what dimension to use, thus more fully specifying the problem, or they discover for themselves which dimensions are available.

To choose the dimensions for analysis, it helps if you have some background with this kind of message. You will have an existing knowledge structure to draw from, which will give you context to understand the nature of this particular message. In addition, in the process of developing your knowledge structure you will have had some experience with this kind of message. For example, if you receive a message from a good friend, you can quickly tell when that friend is trying to be sarcastic or sincere. However, if you received the same message from someone you hardly knew, many of the statements might puzzle you, and you might not know whether to laugh or be offended. When you have little history with a person, you have no knowledge structure to draw from to help you decide what the sender's intended meaning is. When you are unsure of the author's intended meaning, it is difficult to decide whether a statement is significant or trivial.

Analytical dimension
The category for all the components; a continuum that underlies all the components.

The key to completing this second step is to make sure that the **analytical dimensions** you selected will fulfill your purpose for the analysis. Sometimes an analytical dimension is fascinating, but that dimension may have no relevance to your purpose for conducting the analysis. In this case, you could either (a) drop the interesting dimension and find one that is more appropriate to achieve your initial purpose, or (b) change your purpose to fit your selected dimension. Do not ignore option (b). Sometimes we learn that there is a better purpose for the analysis only when we are well into the analysis itself. Thus these first two steps can work together in a cycle.

Step 3: Identify Elements

The third step is to use the dimension(s) to identify the full set of mutually exclusive elements. These are the components of the message. You find them by breaking the message down along your selected analytical dimension. The dimension is your mental template. As you sort through the message and identify relevant elements, you plug them into your template until all the elements are identified and plugged in and the template is full. For example, let's say you are given the problem of analyzing the message of the television series *Friends* along the dimension of characters. You would watch some episodes and notice that there are six continuing characters (Rachel, Monica, Phoebe, Ross, Chandler, and Joey) who appear in every episode, and there is a long list of peripheral characters (parents, other friends, co-workers, bosses, romantic interests) who appear in only one or a few episodes.

Components in a message are like puzzle pieces. You keep picking up pieces and fitting them together until all the pieces are in the puzzle and it is completed. The puzzle pieces are the components that together complete the puzzle by filling out the analytical dimension.

As a metaphor, putting a puzzle together is not exactly right for component analysis. Pieces of a puzzle have a physical shape and color that help you see how they fit together. These clues are missing in the elements of a message. Thus a component analysis is usually more challenging than opening a box of cardboard pieces and putting them together to match the picture on the cover of the box. The cardboard puzzle usually has more pieces than a component analysis, but with a cardboard puzzle you are already given the complete set of pieces as well as the picture of the solved puzzle, and this makes it a fully specified problem. With most component analyses, you have to figure out many aspects for yourself: the analytical dimension, what the pieces are, how many pieces there are, how they fit together, and what picture they will form. However, when you accomplish this, it is very satisfying.

The more you practice analysis, the better you will be at meeting its challenges. With practice comes experience with the type of message as well as with formally developing the skill of analysis. The more experience you have, the more confident you will become. Please try Exercise 4.1 for component analysis to start developing your skills and confidence.

EXERCISE 4.1

PRACTICE AT COMPONENT ANALYSIS

1. Analyze the front page of a newspaper.
   Purpose: To determine how space is used on the front page of a newspaper
   Dimension: Space components. Before beginning your analysis, list the things that you would expect to find on the front page of a newspaper. For example, you might list headlines, stories, pictures, picture captions, graphics, etc. This list will get you started on a component analysis by focusing you on what to look for. However, as you conduct the actual analysis, you may find other components you did not expect to find. Add these other components to your list as you progress through your analysis.
   Process: Go through the message (the front page of a newspaper) and systematically identify all components. When you have finished with one message, find another and analyze it to see if there are other components to add to your list.
   Product: When you finish, you will have a list of all the components that are found on the front pages of newspapers.

2. Again, analyze the front page of a newspaper.
   Purpose: To determine what kinds of stories are featured on the front page of a newspaper
   Dimension: Types of stories. The challenge in this exercise is to clarify the dimension for the analysis, because there are several types of story dimensions. One story dimension is proximity to the place where the newspaper is published (i.e., local, regional, national, and international stories). Another story dimension is kind of content in the stories (such as political, economic, crime, accidents, disasters, etc.). Think of several different story dimensions, and conduct an analysis on each one.
   Process: Go through the message (the front page of a newspaper) and systematically identify all components (types of stories). When you have finished with one message, find another and analyze it to see if there are other components to add to your list.
   Product: When you finish, you will have a list of all the types of stories that are found on the front pages of newspapers.

3. Analyze the building in which a college class is held.
   Purpose: To determine how space is used in the building
   Dimension: Types of space usage. Before beginning your analysis, list the types of usages of space that you might expect to find. For example, you could list classrooms, bathrooms, offices, lounges, etc.
   Process: Walk through the building and systematically identify all components. When you have finished with one message (a building), find another and analyze it to see if there are other components to add to your list.
   Product: When you finish, you will have a list of all the types of space usage in college classroom buildings.

4. Again, analyze the building in which a college class is held.
   Purpose: To determine the physical materials used
   Dimension: Types of building materials. Before beginning your analysis, list the types of usages of materials that you might expect to find. For example, you could list bricks, mortar, wood, rug, ceiling tile, glass, etc.
   Process: Walk through the building and systematically identify all components. When you have finished with one message (a building), find another and analyze it to see if there are other components to add to your list.
   Product: When you finish, you will have a list of all the types of materials that are used in college classroom buildings.

5. Analyze popular music.
   Purpose: To determine different types of popular music
   Dimension: The challenge in this exercise is to think up the dimensions for yourself.
   Process: Begin with the typical music genres that you have heard about (such as rock, rap, country, etc.). Then brainstorm about other possible popular music dimensions. To help your brainstorming, think about the categories used in music award shows, such as the Grammys.
   Product: Try to draw a picture illustrating how all the types of popular music fit together. One type of picture might be a pie graph with each slice labeled as a different type of music. (How many slices would there be? Which would be the bigger slices? Which slices would be next to each other?) Or perhaps your picture would be a guitar with each part labeled as a different type of music. Be creative! Use metaphors!

6. Analyze colleges.
   Purpose: To determine different types of colleges
   Dimension: The challenge in this exercise is to think up the dimensions for yourself.
   Process: Brainstorm about possible dimensions that you could use to conduct a component analysis of colleges. Then pick one dimension and do a component analysis on colleges within a 100-mile radius.
   Product: When you finish, you will have a list of all the types of colleges there are in your surrounding area.

OUTLINE ANALYSIS

⬤ **utline analysis** begins the same way as component analysis, but it goes one step further. It requires you to identify how the components are positioned relative to one another, that is, which components are the organizing components and which are nested within the organizing components. Thus you need to look for components within components. Not all components may be on the same level; some components may be sub-components or sub-sub-components. In an outline analysis, not only are the components important, but the **position** of the components is also important.

To illustrate an outline analysis, let's consider an automobile and think only along the physical dimension. At the general level, all automobiles have the physical components of interior, exterior, and engine plant. We can break the interior down into dashboard, seats, roof, and floor. We can also break the dashboard down into instrument panel, glove compartment, and stereo system. We can break the instrument panel down into fuel gauge, speedometer, odometer, tachometer, oil gauge, battery gauge, and engine temperature gauge. We can break the fuel gauge down into needle and level indicators. We've done a five-level analysis. The beginning point was the car. The first level of the analysis broke down the car into the interior, exterior, and engine; the second level broke down the interior into its components; the third level broke the dashboard into its components; the fourth level broke down the instrument panel; and the fifth level broke the fuel gauge down. See Figure 4.1 for an outline of this analysis. Note that this example is only a partial analysis—it follows only one branch down five levels. A full analysis would break down each component and each sub-component.

How far should an analysis go? It is impossible to give a number of levels as a general answer to this question, but there is a heuristic to guide you. See the identifying number of levels heuristic discussed later in this chapter.

Please try the exercises for outline analysis to continue developing your skills and confidence (Exercise 4.2).

Outline analysis
A multileveled component analysis where some components are categories for other components.

Position
The location of a component relative to other components in an outline analysis.

The Process of Outline Analysis

1. Determine your purpose for the analysis.
2. Select the most appropriate dimension(s) to fulfill your purpose.
3. Use the dimension to look for the full set of mutually exclusive elements on that dimension.
4. Determine how many levels you want or need in your analysis.
5. For each level, search for sub-components to find a full set of mutually exclusive sub-components.

Figure 4.1 Illustration of an outline analysis.

Automobile

I. Interior
   A. Dashboard
      1. Instrument panel
         a. Fuel gauge
            1. Needle
            2. Fuel level indicators
         b. Speedometer
         c. Odometer
         d. Tachometer
         e. Oil gauge
         f. Battery gauge
         g. Engine temperature gauge
      2. Glove compartment
      3. Stereo system
   B. Seats
   C. Roof
   D. Floor
II. Exterior
III. Engine Plant

EXERCISE 4.2

PRACTICE AT OUTLINE ANALYSIS

1. Analyze the building in which a college class is held (this exercise builds on #3 of Exercise 4.1).
   Purpose: To determine how space is used in the building
   Dimension: Types of space usage. Before beginning your analysis, list the types of usage of space that you might expect to find. For example, you could list classrooms, bathrooms, offices, lounges, etc. But for the outline analysis, you also need to think of how these elements can be organized into groups. For example, you might group the elements into public spaces and private spaces, or you could group by floor, or you could group by size of space. When deciding on which grouping scheme to use, think about the purpose of the analysis and what scheme would be most useful to achieve that purpose.

   In this exercise, the purpose statement is intentionally very general so that you can think about what a specific purpose might be. Who might really ask you to do such an exercise in the real world (the fire marshal, the director of maintenance, an architect planning a renovation, a handicapped person)? Let that additional information guide you to narrow down the purpose statement. With a more specific purpose, you have more direction to guide you in selecting a grouping scheme.

Levels: In this exercise, use only two levels. One of these levels is components and the other is groups of components.

Process: Walk through the building and systematically identify all components and groups of components. When you have finished with one message (one building), find another and analyze it to see if there are other components or groups to add to your list. Also, make sure that all components you identify fit into one and only one of your groups, so that your groupings are mutually exclusive.

Product: When you finish, you will have a two-level outline of the components in the college building.

2. Analyze a chapter in a textbook
    Purpose: To determine the structure of information on a particular topic
    Dimension: The challenge in this exercise is to think up the dimensions for yourself. If this is an introductory level textbook by a mainstream American publisher, it is likely that the structure is presented very clearly with layout conventions, type faces, font sizes, color, etc.
    Levels: Allow the message to determine how many levels you will use. However, to make this exercise meaningful, go down at least two levels; to make this exercise manageable, do not go down more than four levels.
    Process: Systematically scan through the chapter to identify all components and groups of components.
    Product: When you finish, you will have a detailed outline of the chapter in a textbook.

3. Analyze a newspaper article (choose one at least 10 column inches long)
    Purpose: To determine the structure of information in the article
    Dimension: The challenge in this exercise is to think up the dimensions for yourself.
    Levels: Allow the message to determine how many levels you will use. However, to make this exercise meaningful, go down at least two levels; to make this exercise manageable, do not go down more than four levels.
    Process: Systematically scan through the article to identify all components and groups of components.
    Product: When you finish, you will have a detailed outline of the newspaper article.

FOCAL PLANE ANALYSIS

The phrase "focal plane" comes from photography. It refers to the plane of objects in a photograph that are most sharply in focus; the objects closer—as well as farther away—are fuzzy and appear to be out of focus. When you take a picture of your family in your backyard, you pose everyone in a group about the same distance from the camera. Then you adjust the lens (or the camera does this automatically) so that their faces are in sharp focus. It does not matter that the background of trees, swing sets, and other houses is not in focus, because they are less important. The picture is of your family, not the other things. When people look at the picture, they see all the other things, but you want them to pay most attention to your family—the elements in the focal plane.

When you encounter a message, there could be lots of information in it, and that information usually exists at different depths. You could focus your analysis on the surface, ignoring deeper things, or you could focus at a particular depth and ignore what is on the surface of the message. Have you ever heard someone say, "You are way too analytical!" This is usually a reaction to someone getting carried away and trying to break things down too far or look too deep. On the other hand, you may have heard someone say, "You have only scratched the surface." This means the person has not done enough analysis.

On which of the depths should you focus your analysis? That depends on your purpose. If you want to analyze a movie for its plot, you can stay pretty much on the surface and describe the obvious plot points. If instead you wanted to analyze the movie to identify elements that reflect a cultural bias of some kind, you would need to focus your analysis at a deeper level of meaning and look at aspects of the characters (such as their gender, their ethnicity, their attractiveness, etc.), how the characters are cast and costumed, what lines they are given, what emotions they portray, what conflicts they encounter, how they resolve those conflicts, and so forth.

Focal plane analysis

Searching for a particular fact or idea in a message.

Focal plane analysis is different from the two types of analyses described above. They require you to consider all the information in the message (at a given level of generality, all components should be accounted for, and those components should be mutually exclusive), whereas focal plane analysis begins with a question, and your task is to search the message to find the one bit of information that answers the question. For example, let's say you hear a word you don't recognize. So you go to the dictionary with the intention of finding the meaning of that word. Do you read through the dictionary to find out how many words are there and how they are arranged? Of course not—you are interested in doing a focal plane analysis of the dictionary, so you search for the page with your word and skip all other pages. Other pages are irrelevant to your focal plane analysis, so you ignore them. You focus only on the one word you care about.

When you are doing a term paper for a course, you typically will do many focal plane analyses. Once you have decided what your thesis statement is (i.e., what your paper is about), you need to find evidence to support your thesis. So you go to databases in the library or on the Internet to find key facts and quotations. When you pick up a book that deals with your topic, you don't read every chapter. You focus only on the chapter that is relevant to your purpose. In that chapter, you don't need to read every word. You scan through the chapter and slow down only when you start recognizing facts that have relevance to your paper.

Some books, especially reference books, are organized to help you conduct your focal plane analysis efficiently. The dictionary arranges words alphabetically, which helps you enormously in finding your word easily. Think how difficult finding your word in a dictionary would be if you did not understand the idea of the alphabet! Fortunately, you have a knowledge structure that tells you that the words in a dictionary are arranged alphabetically and also tells you what the alphabetical order is. You can use the information in this knowledge structure to find your word quickly in the dictionary.

Most books and message vehicles do not arrange their words, facts, or quotations alphabetically. Therefore, you need another knowledge structure to help you navigate through them to find what you need. For example, when you pick up a newspaper to find out whether your favorite team won its game last night, you use a different knowledge structure to guide your focal analysis. You know that the information in a newspaper is not ordered alphabetically; it is ordered thematically in sections. There is usually a front section with the hard news, then a local news section, a business section, a sports section, and a classified ads section. Within the sports section there is a further thematic ordering: longer stories of the most important games on the first page, then shorter and shorter stories on less important events (and more space devoted to ads) as you page through the section. Information on an important playoff game for the local team in a popular professional sport is likely to be on the front page of the sports section. The score of a team in a recreational bowling league will typically be one line in a long list of bowling scores near the end of the sports section. You use your knowledge of how newspapers are organized to direct your attention to the one section, page, and part of the page that contains the element of information you want. You do not need to read through the entire newspaper to find that one bit of information.

The algorithm for focal plane analysis has three steps. First, you need to have a clear purpose. This is often in the form of a question. The more specific the question, the more directed your search will be. Second, you need to access your knowledge structure to find keys to the way information is arranged in the message. The better you can do this, the more quickly you can get through all the individual elements in a message to find the one or two you really need. Also, the better you do this, the more accurate your identification of the key elements will be. (Remember that your goal is both efficiency and accuracy.) Third, you use these keys as a guide to locate the answer to your question.

How can you develop efficiency and accuracy? The answer is to learn more about how information is organized in different types of messages. If you are highly field independent, you will likely have more knowledge about these methods of organization, because you see the big picture and know how to navigate around in all the details. Also, the more context you have about a given message, the more quickly you will be able to move through it. For example, let's say you are assigned to read *Moby Dick* and to answer some questions about it, with one of those questions being something like: What happens to Captain Ahab when he physically confronts Moby Dick? If you've never read the book and have never

---

The Process of Focal Plane Analysis

1. Determine the question to guide the focal plane analysis.
2. Look for keys to the arrangement of information in the message.
3. Use these keys to find the focal plane—the place in the message where the answer resides.

heard of Captain Ahab and don't even know that Moby Dick is a whale, it will take you a long time to find the answer to this question. You must read almost the entire book, starting at the very beginning. However, if you had read the book before and are quite familiar with the story, then you have a great deal of pre-existing knowledge, and you will be able to find the passage you need fairly quickly and furthermore have a high degree of confidence that the passage you identify is the one with the accurate answer to the question.

Please try the exercises for focal plane analysis to continue developing your skills and confidence (Exercise 4.3).

EXERCISE 4.3

PRACTICE AT FOCAL PLANE ANALYSIS

1. Analyze Chapter 3 of this book.
   Questions:
   - What is meant by maturation?
   - How can you tell if someone is field dependent?
   - What is a knowledge style?

   Process: Scan quickly through the chapter and notice the headings and sub-headings. Find the section of the chapter that is most likely to contain the answer to your particular question. Read carefully through that section until you find the answer to the question.

   Product: Short factual answers to the above questions.

2. Analyze Chapter 2 of this book.
   Question: What is the difference between critical thinking and strategic thinking?

   This is a more difficult question than the questions in the previous exercise, because the chapter does not provide an answer that you could quote (i.e., it is not expressed in one set of words). Instead you need to patch together ideas from several paragraphs to arrive at a good answer to this question.

   Process: Scan quickly through the chapter and notice the headings and sub-headings. Find the section of the chapter that is most likely to contain the answer to your particular question. Read carefully through those sections until you find relevant pieces of information. Assemble those pieces together into an answer.

   Product: A paragraph where you (a) describe what critical thinking and strategic thinking are, then (b) explain the difference.

3. Analyze a newspaper article on a controversy.
   Questions:
   - How many sides are there to this controversy?
   - Who are the prominent figures (people or organizations) on each side of this controversy?
   - What are the main arguments presented by the prominent figures on each side?
   - What is new in the controversy, that is, what happened that made this newsworthy?

Process: Read the article. Look for particular claims, quotations, and facts that would answer each of the questions.

Keys: The more you know about journalism and the more experience you have in reading newspaper stories, the more you bring to this assignment. You should know that journalists typically put the most important information in the lead, which is the first few sentences of the article. So, the element of newsworthiness should be present in the first sentence or two. Also, journalists try to be "fair," and this means that when they write about a controversy, they acknowledge all sides. Journalists use quotations to illustrate the position of each side and attribute those quotes to prominent figures.

Product: A short paragraph for each question.

HEURISTICS

The algorithms discussed above are rules that apply to just about any analysis task. However, those algorithms might not be enough to complete the analysis. If you have a partially specified problem, you will need to fill in some of the gaps on your own. The four heuristics below can help.

Analysis Heuristic 1: Defining the Purpose

A good analysis starts with a clear purpose. This allows you to look for logical dimensions that will fulfill that purpose. Often, this is very easy to do. Sometimes you are given the purpose and the dimensions. For example, a teacher may give you a homework assignment to analyze a novel by its plot. You might have trouble actually finding the plot points, but at least you know what to look for—you have been given the dimension for the analysis.

There are also times when the purpose for the analysis is not clear. You might hear a message and want to understand it better. In this case, you want to analyze the message, but you lack a clear purpose. For example, you may watch a movie and wonder why you like it so much; you want to understand your reaction better and so are motivated to analyze the movie, but you are not clear on a purpose. Or you may hear a speaker argue a particular point of view and feel uncomfortable with the argument; you want to analyze it, but again the specific purpose is not clear. Or you may read a news story in a magazine, and something about it does not seem right. In these examples—as in many others—you are motivated to understand the message better, but you are not sure what your specific purpose would be in an analysis. When this happens, the algorithm by itself is not enough. You need some more guidance: a **purpose-defining heuristic.**

If you do not have a clear purpose for an analysis, you cannot complete the first step in the algorithm. It can be helpful to skip to Step 2 in the algorithm and list all possible dimensions along which you could conduct the analysis. Seeing the range of options will help you focus on the dimensions that seem to be most useful. Selecting a dimension first can help bring to the surface what your purpose is for the analysis.

Purpose-defining heuristic

A guideline to help specify a purpose for the analysis when one is not given.

Generic dimension

A dimension (such as structure or function) that can be used for a component analysis of almost anything.

Structural dimension

Physical properties of the components of a message.

Functional dimension

Purpose or usage of the components of a message.

Remember that people with well-developed knowledge structures on the topic of a message are better able to identify all possible dimensions for an analysis. But what do you do when the topic is new to you and you have no existing knowledge structure? In this case, remember that most messages lend themselves to being analyzed along the **generic dimensions** of **structure** and **function.** For example, let's say you want to analyze a television news program. When you think about the structure of the show, you can see the component elements: news anchor talking head, remote feed with a reporter talking at the scene, stock footage of background material, superimposed graphics, and pictures. When you break the story down functionally, you find elements designed to inform the audience (appeals to the intellect) and elements designed to entertain the audience (appeal to emotions). Another example is an automobile. You could analyze any automobile structurally by identifying its major components (exterior, interior, engine), as we did earlier in this chapter. You can also analyze automobiles by their function (transportation, safety, efficiency).

Thinking about generic dimensions is a good way to get started, but it is not a good place to stop. Once you are warmed up by thinking about generic dimensions, continue to explore other dimensions of the message you want to analyze. Most messages offer other dimensions for analysis beyond the structural and functional ones. For example, you could analyze automobiles in terms of class (car, truck, SUV, etc.) and price. You could analyze a television news story conceptually, looking for the ideas in the story—the who, what, when, where, why, and how. You could analyze a political treatise by type of appeal (ethos, pathos, logos); a situation comedy by type of humor; a series on real-life crimes by types of crimes portrayed and types of perpetrators; a mathematical equation by types of transformation (addition, subtraction, division, square root, etc.) or branch of mathematics (trigonometry, geometry, algebra, calculus, etc.); a musical concert by types of instruments used; fossils by time period.

Settling on a purpose after you have assessed all the possible dimensions for analysis has several advantages. First, it is likely to help you expand your purpose by using more than one dimension in your analysis. Second, it can give you confidence that you have made a reasoned choice of dimension. You will then be more likely to be committed to conducting a quality analysis.

Analysis Heuristic 2: Inductively Derived Dimensions

What do you do when you cannot identify a dimension to guide your analysis? Don't get frustrated and give up; instead get started with the analysis and try to derive a useful dimension **inductively.**

Inductively derived dimension heuristic

A guideline for inferring a dimension by listing characteristics of the message.

For example, let's say you hear someone speak about an issue and take a clear position. You have never heard anything about this particular issue before, but it fascinates you, and you want to analyze the issue so you can understand it better. In this case, a structural or functional analysis would not make much sense, because you know nothing about the issue other than what this one speaker has said. Therefore, you don't know how many positions there are on that issue or the nature of those positions. Breaking the speaker's ideas down into components will not tell you what the components of the issue itself are. You need to find some dimension that is broader than this one message; then you will be able to position this one message somewhere on the broader dimension. How do you get started?

The simplest way to start is to determine if the person is arguing *for* or *against* the issue itself. The pro and con become the poles on the dimension, which is the issue itself. Then you need to think about whether there is one or more middle or compromise positions. By thinking of some middle positions, you are constructing a dimension (the positions on the issue) from a message that provides information on only one position. The next step is to go to the library or the Internet to find out if the positions you inferred do in fact exist. When you find information on those other positions, you can do a focal plane analysis on those messages to identify the essence of each of those positions. The more you read and think about the issue, the better you can refine your analytical dimension by adding new positions, dropping others, and collapsing several inferred positions into one position.

You may find deriving positions inductively to be challenging. The need for it mainly arises when you are in a new area where you do not have much prior knowledge. This is one reason why it is more difficult to learn about a new topic than to increase your learning on a familiar topic. Meeting the challenge and being willing to do the work are necessary if you wish to expand your learning.

Don't give up on an analysis when you can't find a good dimension to begin. Rather than let this barrier stop you, think laterally to get around it. Infer a dimension, use it as a tentative guide to position the current message, then look for evidence of other inferred positions on that dimension.

Here is an example of the entire process. Let's say you decide to analyze your ideal conception of a romantic partner. You have a fuzzy idea about what it might be, and you want to analyze it so you can understand it better. You could begin by listing some of the qualities that your ideal romantic partner should have. Let's say you list the following characteristics: tall, athletic, dark hair, and green eyes.

Notice that all of these are physical characteristics. Thus you can infer a physical dimension from this particular list of characteristics—this is a dimension that underlies all the characteristics in your list. Now ask yourself, are there other physical characteristics that you like—such as a smile, dimples, shape of lips, and so forth? Are there physical things you don't like? List them along the physical dimension.

Can you think of other dimensions? After all, the physical, while important, is only one dimension. If you use only one dimension for your ideal romantic partner, you might wind up with a partner who is good to look at but intolorable in other ways. How about adding another dimension to your analysis—perhaps the dimension of personality? Think of all the personality characteristics that you really like and don't like in a romantic partner.

When you started this analysis of your ideal conception of a romantic partner, no one gave you the dimensions to use. You had to infer them on your own. You inferred the first dimension, physical characteristics, by asking yourself what the items on your initial list had in common. This dimension triggered your thinking about other possible dimensions, such as personality.

Analysis Heuristic 3: Identifying Number of Elements

How many elements should be identified as positions along an analytical dimension? The answer varies according to how many obvious positions are on a given dimension and how much detail is in the message you are analyzing. It also varies according to your conceptual differentiation ability. Those who have a strong drive to differentiate conceptually are likely to have many categories and sub-categories, while those who do not have a high motivation to differentiate may have few.

Number of elements heuristic

A guideline for deciding how many elements are on an analytical dimension.

Instead of looking for some magic **number of elements,** be guided by the *range* and the *gaps* in your analysis. When you think about the range, are you satisfied that you have examined the message for elements at both extreme ends of the dimension(s)? Are there gaps along the dimension, where you have not found elements? If so, are there really no elements to fit those gaps, or have you missed something?

As an example, let's use this book as a message and analyze it along the dimension of structural organization. Let's say we list front matter, preface, and four chapters. That would be a good start, but it leaves out some components—Chapters 5 through 12, as well as the index. For a complete analysis, we need to include those other components. As another example, let's say instead that we list front matter; title page; acknowledgments; preface; introductory chapter; chapter on strategic thinking; chapter on knowledge styles; chapters on filtering, processing, and sharing; and index. This too is faulty, because the elements in the list are not mutually exclusive; the title page and the acknowledgments are part of the front matter. This list includes a full set of major components but also sub-components of one of those major components. If the analysis is to go to two levels—with components as well as sub-components—then the major components need to be presented as a full set and the sub-components need to be presented as a full set of each major component. This goes beyond a relatively simple component analysis and into outline analysis.

Analysis Heuristic 4: Identifying Number of Levels

Number of levels heuristic

A guideline for deciding how many levels an outline analysis should contain.

How far should an analysis go—how many **levels** should it include? The answer lies in your purpose. Remember, analysis is a tool. When you use this tool, you must have some purpose in mind. With a relatively minor purpose, one level of analysis may be sufficient—it is better to do some analysis than to accept the surface meaning, but it is not worth spending a great deal of effort if the issue is of relatively minor importance to you.

If you are trying to understand an important problem, you will probably want your analysis to reach the root of the problem. Of course, once you reach this point, there is little reason to continue to deeper levels; this would be "over-analyzing" the problem. For example, automobile mechanics who are investigating why a car won't run will typically analyze the car beginning with the engine plant. When they break the car down into the components of interior, exterior, and engine plant, they ignore the interior and exterior—no need to study any sub-levels of those components. Given the purpose of the analysis, it makes sense only to conduct the analysis on the component of the engine plant. Mechanics then rule out the sub-components that are functioning well, and continue the analysis to deeper levels of those sub-components that appear to be faulty. When they find the unit that is faulty, they stop the analysis and replace the faulty unit.

The key to a good outline analysis is to have a complete set of components at each level and to know the structure—which sub-components are nested within each component. You will continue to break components down into sub-components (differentiating concepts) until you achieve the purpose of the analysis.

AVOIDING TRAPS

Achieving your purpose is like traveling along a path. Along the way, you may encounter **traps.** If you get caught in one, it will be difficult to reach your destination.

Trap
A barrier along the problem-solving path that can stop you from achieving your purpose.

Many of these traps are emotional ones. When you undertake an analysis—or work with any of the other seven skills to be discussed—your emotions can pull you into a trap where you feel frustrated and cannot find a way out. If you can't gain control over your emotions, then you can't get out of such a trap. To escape such a trap, you must pay attention to your emotions and harness their energy. For example, if an analysis turns out to be particularly difficult, let yourself get angry. Anger can be a positive motivator. It increases your heart rate and blood pressure, and this translates into energy. Anger also increases your ability to concentrate. However, you must *control* that energy and focus it on the task at hand rather than directing it toward other people, yourself, or the situation. If you cannot control and direct your anger, it will take you away from your task and become a barrier to your success. If instead you can direct your anger, you can use its energy to work through the challenge and be successful.

Don't be afraid to fight back against dense or seemingly nonsensical information. Argue against it. Let yourself laugh out loud when something appears ridiculous. And when you have finished a particularly hard analysis, give your book a high five. This might sound silly, but you should always reward yourself in some way when you are finished so that you feel good about what you have done.

Never leave a problem when you are feeling defeated by it. Instead get angry and energized. Work through the problem until you feel more positive about what you are doing, and *then* stop if you need to. Take your breaks when you are feeling good and successful (or at least hopeful), so that you will want to come back to work after the break. If you take your breaks when you feel bad and defeated, you remain in the trap and it will be more difficult to get back to work. Monitor your emotions so you can control them and become more successful.

CONCLUSION

It is possible to encounter a message without analyzing it. We frequently do just that. For example, you might read an entire newspaper article or watch an entire movie without analyzing it; you could experience a message superficially as a monolithic whole. You would experience the movie as some good guys trying to stop some bad guys from committing crimes. When you do this, your unit of experience (and hence memory of it) is very superficial, that is, it has no depth of detail. You are not aware of the many steps in the plot; you do not recognize unique characters and their contributions to the plot; you do not appreciate the production elements of editing, lighting, sound, music, costuming, and sets. Living your life this way would be terribly boring.

You can analyze something in various ways. One way is to do a component analysis, where you identify elements along some dimension. A second way is to do an outline analysis, where you identify the structure of a message by looking for its components and sub-components. A third way is focal plane analysis, where you begin with a specific question and search through the message to find the answer. This chapter presented algorithms that you can use to conduct each of these three types of analysis.

Many of the analytical tasks you encounter are partially specified, so in order to complete all the steps in a given analysis, you also need to use heuristics. This chapter presented four heuristics. These guidelines can help you (1) define the purpose of the analysis when it is not given to you; (2) find positions on analytical dimensions when those dimensions are not provided in the problem; (3) identify the number of elements on a dimension when the number is not specified prior to the analysis; and (4) identify the number of levels an outline analysis needs to deal with in order to achieve its purpose.

The more carefully you conduct an analysis, the better the result will be, whether it is a list of components, a structured outline, or the answer to a question. This result then becomes the raw material that you will use in applying the other seven skills of strategic thinking.

CHAPTER 5

Skill 2: Evaluation

LEARNING OBJECTIVES

By reading this chapter, you will:

1. Learn how to develop your skill of evaluation.
2. Understand how to use two types of heuristics to help you with the skill of evaluation.
   - Category construction
   - Multiple elements
3. Understand how to avoid nine traps that can prevent you from using the skill of evaluation well.
   - Too limited a standard
   - Too much trust in knowledge structure
   - Neglecting credibility of source
   - Misinterpreting percentages
   - Misunderstanding causal relationships
   - Misconstruing comparative claims
   - Underdeveloped abilities
   - Underdeveloped knowledge structures
   - Misunderstanding the role of emotions

Evaluating means assessing the worth of an element. Assessing the value of something essentially requires comparing an element to a standard. Recall from the previous chapter that analysis is the skill used to sift through the message to identify its elements—components, the arrangement of components, or a fact. Evaluation uses the elements generated in the analysis as raw material. Therefore, you must analyze before you can perform an evaluation.

It is possible, of course, to encounter a message without evaluating it, but then you have no option but to accept the message as it is. For example, you can read an entire magazine article without ever considering its accuracy or its value to you. You might simply assume that the information in the message is accurate—why else would a respected magazine publish it?

Evaluating requires a skeptical approach, the attitude that elements might not always be accurate or useful for your needs. This skepticism is often referred to as *critical thinking, critical viewing,* or just *critical.* When people talk about a "critical analysis," they usually mean an "evaluation," because they are referring to the challenging of elements or arguments.

THE EVALUATION ALGORITHM

The evaluation algorithm has five steps. The steps are presented here in a certain order, but in practice you might want to repeat steps because a particular evaluation calls for it. However, it is best to do the steps in the following order to begin with, then deviate when you have a good reason.

Step 1: Select a Standard

Standard

A benchmark that is used to compare elements. Elements that meet the standard are judged as satisfactory, elements that fall short of the standard are failures, and elements that exceed the standard are judged as excelling.

Cognitive standard

A benchmark used to judge factual material.

The first step in an evaluation is to select a **standard** for assessing the value of your message elements. Often we select a standard without much thought, or we use a standard purely out of habit. However, when the evaluation task is an important one, it is better to spend some time considering your range of options for a standard rather than quickly accepting the first standard that pops into your head.

There are four kinds of standards: cognitive, moral, emotional, and aesthetic. **Cognitive standards** are the benchmarks that make something satisfying to the mind. A popular cognitive standard is accuracy. We all want facts to be accurate. You can compare an element to what you already know about a topic. If the new element does not fit with what you already know, then you would judge the new element to be inaccurate. However, the limitation of this procedure is that your standard might be the thing that is inaccurate. Therefore, it is good to use an external standard for accuracy (see "Avoiding Traps" later in this chapter).

Another cognitive standard is utility. To use the standard of utility, you need an understanding of your existing knowledge structures. By looking at the way your knowledge is arranged, you can decide whether you need the new element that you are evaluating. You ask yourself if this new element is something you would find useful to incorporate into your existing knowledge structures.

The Skill of Evaluation

Purpose: To assess the worth of an element
Pre-Task: Conduct an analysis to identify message elements.
Process:

1. Select a standard for the evaluation.
2. Determine the most appropriate criteria set(s) for each standard.
3. Select elements.
4. Compare an element to each criterion in the criteria set and make a judgment about whether:
   A. the element matches the criterion (acceptable)
   B. the element exceeds the criterion (excellence)
   C. the element falls short of the criterion (failure)
5. Construct a summary judgment about the value of the element.
   A. If the element receives a uniform judgment on all criteria, then the summary judgment is the same as any one of the judgments on the individual criteria.
   B. If the element does not receive a uniform judgment on all criteria, then weight the criteria in terms of relative importance and use your judgments on the weightiest criteria to influence most the construction of your summary judgment.

A new element can have utility in three ways. First, it could extend your knowledge structure by becoming a new element on a new topic, thus broadening your knowledge structure. Second, it could become a new element in an already existing knowledge structure, to extend its depth. Third, it could become an additional example of a fact you already have in your knowledge structure. This adds weight to that point.

For example, let's say you are planning to go to Cancun for your next spring break and you have a newly formed Cancun knowledge structure with very little detail. You get some brochures and extend your knowledge structure by adding information about beaches, hotels, night clubs, and so forth. Based on the information you have, you decide to stay at the Hotel del Extreme, but you keep looking for more information about this hotel to deepen your knowledge structure on this particular topic. Finally, you talk to people who stayed at the Hotel del Extreme last spring break, and each person tells you how great it was. This new information is repetitive, but it serves to make your decision to stay at that hotel weightier and thus more settled and less likely to change. All of this information has utility for you, but in different ways: some of it expands the range of topics in your knowledge structure, some deepens the detail on one topic, some adds strength and weight to a particular element or decision.

In addition to cognitive standards, there are **moral standards,** which are the benchmarks that make something satisfying to a person's code of ethics or religion. Many people are offended by television shows with violence, foul language, and promiscuous sex, because these shows fail to live up to the viewers' moral standards.

Emotional standards are expectations that a message should evoke a particular emotional reaction. For example, people often go to horror films in order to feel fear to a higher degree than they have ever felt before. The expectation for a certain level of fear is the standard; movies that do not live up to this standard are judged as disappointments.

Aesthetic standards are the benchmarks people use to judge the artistic quality of a message. For example, when we evaluate a movie, we can focus on the artistic ability evidenced by the actors, directors, writers, music composers, editors, costumers, lighting crew, and so forth. The more experience we have watching movies, the more elaborate our aesthetic standards will be. People who engage in the crafts involved in producing movies develop even more refined standards. This is why experienced movie critics are often hard to please. Because they have a great deal of knowledge about good and bad movies, a movie has to exceed standards on many criteria in order to be considered good.

Most evaluations are not simple one-dimensional tasks; instead, multiple standards could be used simultaneously to evaluate a particular message. When people evaluate a movie, they might use any of several standards. Some might focus on characters and plot exclusively. These people have developed standards for characters and plot. If a movie meets those standards—for example, it features their favorite stars and has a strong and satisfying story, they will conclude that the movie was good. Someone else who sees the same movie and has a different set of criteria—for example, a moral theme and an offbeat plot—may judge the movie to be bad. Both people saw the same movie, but they had totally different evaluations of it, because they applied different standards. The judgment of value depends on the standards, so it is important that you be aware of your standards when you begin an evaluation.

Knowledge structures are also very important to the evaluation algorithm. For example, let's say you have an assignment in a business class to read about a company and evaluate its business practices. You will need a good knowledge structure with cognitive elements about accounting procedures so you can read the company's balance sheet and assess the financial health of the company. That knowledge structure will tell you what standard to use. (Should you use revenue, profit, earnings per share, debt to equity ratio, or something else?) Also, you need a knowledge structure with cognitive elements that can help you evaluate the company's marketing plan. (What are reasonable sales projections, has the company priced the products well, is the advertising budget large enough to achieve the goals?) In addition, you could make a moral assessment, if you had a well-developed knowledge structure about business ethics. If you didn't have such a knowledge structure, then you would be forced to make a superficial and intuitive moral assessment without a clear moral

Moral standard

A benchmark indicating what is acceptable from an ethical or religious point of view.

Emotional standard

Expectation for the kind and degree of emotional reaction that should be evoked by a message.

Aesthetic standard

A benchmark used to judge the artistic quality of a message.

standard. In this example, you are not likely to use an emotional or aesthetic standard. Types of standards change depending on the messages and elements you are evaluating.

Step 2: Determine Criteria for Standards

Criteria are the conditions that must be met to achieve the standard. Unless these can be written clearly and with detail, the standard itself may not be useful. For example, let's say you listen to a CD and you judge it to be "cool." This judgment implies that you have made an evaluation on the standard of coolness and that this CD exceeded your minimum criteria for being cool. This judgment may be fine for you, especially if you regard "cool" as an emotional standard and you look for things that trigger that feeling of "cool" in you. However, if you had to explain your evaluation to someone else, it would be difficult to do, because you probably haven't articulated the criteria of coolness. If you were assigned to evaluate the CD for a music appreciation class or to write a music column for a newspaper, you would need to say something beyond, "This is a cool CD." You would need to articulate your criteria for coolness and explain in detail what a CD would have to exhibit in order to meet that criterion.

For another example, think of the grades you earn in your courses. Your performance is labeled as being excellent (A), good (B), average (C), poor (D), or failing (E or F). However, professors almost always give a description of what "A" work, "B" work, and so on consist of. Often these criteria are included in the syllabus at the start of the course. Students want detail—they want to know specifically what the difference between an A and a B is. They want to know in detail what they have to do—the criteria—in order to achieve a particular grade.

On the surface, almost all standards seem to be categorical—that is, with just a few levels or categories, like letter grades—but most are really based on a continuum—such as your numerical grade in a course, anywhere from 0 to 100. The five letters used for grades are categories of performance, but they are not "natural" categories. Typically if your performance reaches or exceeds a criterion of 90 percent, it is given the label of excellent. Excellence in this example is not a category in the sense that being a male or a female is a natural category. Instead, excellence means that your performance has exceeded some minimum point and is now within the range that, according to the criterion, is called "excellent."

When an evaluation is important, think carefully about whether your standard is a set of categories or a continuum. If it is a set of categories, you need to specify criteria—what is required for each category. If instead your standard relies on a continuum, you need to decide two things when establishing your criteria: First, think about how to position the elements on the continuum. What characteristics need to be present in the element to move it up (or down) on the continuum? Second, decide how to label the ranges on the continuum. In the simplest case, you need to label two ranges—acceptable and non-acceptable. At what point on the continuum do you draw the line of acceptability? For example, if you were a professor, where would you draw the lines between grades? Should 90 percent and 99 percent both be labeled as an A? Or should 90 percent be an A–?

Criteria

Conditions that must be met in order to achieve a standard.

Should 90 percent perhaps be a B+ or even a B? These decisions can be difficult, but they must be made. Professors must clearly communicate to students what the standards are and what the criteria are for meeting those standards, in order to be fair.

Step 3: Select Elements

Once you have identified your standard and established your criteria on the standard, you need to select elements in the message that are appropriate to compare to the standard. These elements come from an analysis. If your standard has something to do with the completeness of the information in the message, then the product of a component analysis would be relevant. If your standard has something to do with the clarity or organization of the message, then the product of an outline analysis would seem to be the most appropriate. If your standard were one of the accuracy of a fact quoted in a message, then the product of a focal plane analysis would be the most appropriate.

Step 4: Compare Elements to the Criteria on the Standard

The fourth step is to compare an element to each criterion on the standard and make a judgment about whether: (a) the element matches the criterion and is therefore acceptable; (b) the element exceeds the standard and is therefore judged as excelling; or (c) the element falls short of the criterion and is therefore judged a failure. The simplest type of evaluation to make is one where your purpose is clear, the standard is clear, and the criteria for meeting the standard are clear.

Step 5: Construct a Summary Assessment

This step is required when you have multiple criteria. Of course, if the element exceeds each criterion, then the summary is simple—the element excels. If the element falls short of each criterion, then it is also simple to conclude that the element fails. Thus if the element receives a uniform judgment on all criteria, then the summary judgment is the same as the judgments on the individual criteria.

What do you do when the element exceeds some criteria and falls short on others? This can present a challenge—one that you are likely to confront frequently. For example, you meet someone who you want to evaluate as "dating material." Suppose you have high standards: the person needs (1) to be smart, (2) to have a great personality, and (3) to be fabulously good looking. The person you are evaluating fails on the first two criteria but excels on the third one. On balance, how do you evaluate this person? If all three criteria are equally important, then this person will fail the evaluation as "dating material." However, if criterion #3 is the most important—even more important than the other two criteria combined—then the person will pass the evaluation.

HEURISTICS

I n the evaluation algorithm presented above, there are at least two places where your evaluation task is only partially specified. In those instances, you need to use your own judgment to decide how to proceed and thereby specify the task more fully. These two places are identified below, with heuristics to help you decide what to do when you run into gaps in the evaluation process.

Evaluation Heuristic 1: Constructing Categories

When a standard is a continuum, it's necessary to label ranges of positions as **categories.** You probably do this all the time without thinking about it, but sometimes you will need to think more carefully about how you do this. For example, someone tells you it is 85 degrees today, and you say that it is hot. You have taken the 85 degrees (one particular position on the temperature continuum) and translated it into a category (hot). Few people would find fault with this translation. However, what if someone told you it was 80 degrees? Is that hot? What about 79 degrees? What I am trying to do here is to get you to think about where the boundary is for the category "hot." With some evaluation tasks, defining the boundaries clearly is a very important thing to do. For example, when a professor translates the points you earn in a course (a continuum) into a grade (a category), you want to know exactly where the boundaries are.

Category construction heuristic
Guidelines for dividing a continuum into meaningful categories.

How do you draw these lines in a way that does not seem arbitrary or unfair? To illustrate this problem, let's say you are interested in how news programs cover political candidates. The unit of interest to you is the sound bite—where the candidate is shown on the screen speaking about his or her position on some issue. You have analyzed 10 news programs and identified 25 sound bites. You have measured the length of each sound bite, and they range from three seconds to 90 seconds. You want to evaluate how well the news programs cover candidates' positions, as indicated by how much time they show candidates speaking in their own words. What standard would you use? How would you determine the acceptable length of a sound bite? Are you willing to say that a sound bite of say 20 seconds is long enough to present the candidate, but anything shorter than that is too superficial?

There are three techniques you can consider using to make your dividing lines less arbitrary. First, you could use the same criteria and lines as someone else who has worked on a similar evaluation. The danger here is that the other person may have constructed the criteria poorly, so your use of that design will result in a poor evaluation. In order to avoid perpetuating other people's mistakes, think about whether their criteria seem any less arbitrary and any more meaningful than criteria that you could develop on your own.

A second technique is to find some credible benchmark outside of the evaluation process that could be brought into the process as a way of justifying drawing a line in a particular place. With the sound bite example, perhaps you could find a study that reported that when people are exposed to factual information in messages longer than 30 seconds, their understanding and recall increase dramatically.

If you could find such a research study, then you would have a good reason to draw your line of acceptability at 30 seconds.

A third technique you can use to make your decisions less arbitrary is to avoid drawing those lines until you look at where the elements fall on the standard's continuum. Look at the pattern and notice where the clusters of elements are. Professors often plot the performance of all their students on a continuum, then look at the distribution before they decide on where to draw the line between an A and a B, and so on. Let's say a professor gives an exam to a class of 30 students. A perfect score would be 100 points, and the scores of the 30 students are displayed in Figure 5.1. The highest performance was by a student who earned 94 points, and there is a cluster of 12 students between 94 and 87 points. There is another cluster between 82 and 77 points. In this case, it would not be good to draw the line between an A and a B at 90 percent, because there is little difference between the performances of the 12 students in the cluster from 94 to 87; they all excelled and all should get A's. This group is significantly higher than the 15 students clustered in the range of 82 to 77 points, so these 15 students should all receive the same grade, a step lower than the group of 12 students in the top cluster—they should get B's. Thus, the line between an A and a B should be drawn around 85 percent.

Evaluation Heuristic 2: Multiple Elements

Multiple elements heuristic

Guidelines for making a summary judgment when there are more than one element–standard comparison.

The simplest form of evaluation is to compare only one element to the standard. Sometimes it makes more sense, however, to take more than one element into consideration. For example, let's say you want to evaluate American universities and find the best one for you. Suppose you want to major in journalism. You select a standard of "journalism major." Either a school offers a major in journalism (meets the standard and is therefore acceptable), or it does not (unacceptable). It is relatively easy to evaluate each university according to this standard. Let's say you end up with 100 universities that meet your standard. This is too many universities to apply to, so you decide to get more sophisticated in your evaluation in order to cut the list down to a more manageable number. You choose a different standard: the standard of an "*outstanding* journalism program." In this case, your standard would likely be composed of several elements, such as number of courses (the more the better), number of internship opportunities (the more the better), the quality of internship opportunities (the more prestigious the newspaper and television stations the better), the reputation of the faculty (the more Pulitzer prizes won the better). To consider all these factors, you must use a **standard-complex.**

Standard-complex

A standard that is composed of multiple criteria.

Using a standard-complex is just like using a single standard, but two aspects make it a little more challenging. The first is deciding which elements should be included in the standard-complex. The above example illustrated that there are many ways of evaluating the quality of a journalism program. Which of those elements mentioned would you include? Are there other elements you would add?

The second challenge is making a summary judgment. Should all of the elements have equal weight? If you were choosing journalism school, would all the elements contribute the same amount to the overall evaluation? Maybe one should be more important. Perhaps a certain program has few courses and lim-

Figure 5.1   Example of transforming a continuum of scores to categories.

Points Earned on an Exam			
94			
93			
92			
91	91		
90	90		
89	89	89	
88			
87			
82			
81	81	81	
80	80	80	
79	79		
78	78	78	78
77	77		
72			
68			
61			

ited internship possibilities, but it has one faculty member who has won three Pulitzer prizes and who is an excellent mentor. In this case, the quality of one faculty member can be strong enough to compensate for shortcomings in all other areas. Your summary judgment might be that the journalism program exceeds your standard.

AVOIDING TRAPS

sing the skill of evaluation is relatively simple if you are organized and systematic. However, some traps can hold you back if you fall into them.

Evaluation Trap 1: Too Limited a Standard

It is important to start evaluations by carefully considering all possible standards. If you intuitively select a standard for the sake of convenience, your evaluation will likely have little use. It is better to explore all the relevant standards across the different types—cognitive, moral, emotional, and aesthetic. It is also wise to incorporate multiple criteria in the standard. This makes the evaluation more complex, but the results will usually be more valuable.

Evaluation Trap 2: Too Much Trust in Existing Knowledge Structures

Although knowledge structures are very useful—they can help you retrieve existing information and make sense of new information—you should not automatically trust them for accuracy. You may have incorporated inaccurate information into your knowledge structure, or perhaps some previously accurate information has become outdated. To keep your knowledge structures as accurate as possible, search continually for new messages on your topics, and keep an open mind when you see new information that contradicts the information you have in your existing knowledge structures.

Let's say you hear a very damaging claim against a political candidate whom you favor. Your existing knowledge structure is probably composed of a large number of positive elements about this candidate. The new claim does not fit into your existing knowledge structure. You must decide whether to believe the new claim and incorporate it into your knowledge base, which would require substantial alterations, or to disregard the claim. There are several techniques you could use to decide what to do—to evaluate the claim. You could use an accuracy standard and examine the credibility of the claim. Is the source of the accusation trustworthy? Does the accusation seem plausible? Another technique is to consider the weight of the claim. Has it been made by just one person? Has anyone else come forth to support it? Is evidence given? If not, the claim has little weight, especially compared to the weight of favorable knowledge you already have about the candidate.

If you disregard all information that does not conform to your existing knowledge structures, then you will have no chance of changing those structures as the world changes. Your thinking becomes out of date and irrelevant when you hold anachronistic beliefs based on now-faulty information. Preserving traditions and being loyal are important, but some people want to protect their old beliefs and perspectives at all costs. When people screen out all discrepant new information, they reinforce the information avoider knowledge style and lose the ability to process information that does not reinforce what they already believe.

Evaluation Trap 3: Neglecting Credibility of Source

Another trap is comparing the message element to the standard without taking into consideration the source of the message. Not all sources are equally **credible.** If you find a fact in a message appearing in the *New York Times* or *Time* magazine, it is likely to be very credible. However, if you see a fact in a story reported in the *National Enquirer,* it is not prudent to regard it as highly credible.

Source credibility

Likelihood that the information presented by a source is accurate.

Be careful of the messages provided by people who are labeled as experts. Ask yourself: What makes this person an expert? Some experts are more expert than others, and being an expert doesn't make a person right. In some areas, such as forecasting the weather or the economy, all experts are wrong most of the time. Economists are always developing sophisticated mathematical models to predict aspects of the stock market or the economy. Some of these models are better at predicting than others, and the authors of these "better" models are regarded as the experts. For example, Harry's model may be right 25 percent of the time, while everyone else's models are right only 20 percent of the time. So Harry is regarded as the leading expert. However, Harry is still wrong most of the time.

Experts benefit from a "halo effect"—that is, we have been conditioned to trust and believe them. Remember that even the best experts are sometimes wrong because of faulty reasoning. It is a good idea to evaluate each claim made by experts to see if this is one of the times they are actually right.

Consider how the information was generated. If you are reading about a public opinion survey, inquire into the reputation of the surveyor, the nature of the sample (who was asked the questions), and especially the wording of the questions. For example, let's say you hear that the president's approval rating has climbed to 70 percent. That sounds pretty good, but what does it really mean? You need to know something about the sample. Was the approval high, but only among people who answered their telephone the evening the poll was taken? Or only among people living in one part of the country? Also you need to know what "approval" means. Does it mean approval of handling the office in terms of domestic issues, foreign policy, or both? Does it mean that the economy is strong, and the president is getting the credit? Or does it mean that people simply like him as a human being? You need to know how the question was asked. Although the following three questions could be used to measure approval of the president, people are likely to provide different answers to each:

1. Do you think the president is doing an excellent job?

2. Do you think the president is doing a satisfactory job?

3. Do you think the president is doing the best job he can, given his limitations?

Finally, you need to know what answer choices were available to the respondents. Did the pollsters give people only two choices (yes or no), or did they allow for the possibility that someone may not have an opinion (yes, no, no opinion), or did they measure degree of support (doing a great job, doing a good job, doing an okay job, doing a bad job)? All of these factors have a significant influence on the result. To accept results without examining the key factors that generated them is to risk being misled.

Evaluation Trap 4: Misinterpreting Percentages

Often facts appear as percentages. These numbers can be especially trouble-some—they may look simple, but they can be misleading. Remember that per-centages are computed from fractions, where one number (the numerator, on the top of the fraction) is compared to another number (the denominator, on the bot-tom of the fraction). To interpret a fraction, you need to know where each of these numbers came from. People often make the error of taking a percentage based on one situation and using it to make a case in a different situation. But since the situations are different, one or both of the numbers in the fraction may no longer be applicable.

To illustrate, let's consider the argument that the divorce rate in this country is now 50 percent. This figure is a percentage, and like all percentages, it is computed from two numbers. What are those numbers? If we compare the number of mar-riages with the number of divorces in any given year, we get a ratio of 2 to 1. In other words, there were twice as many marriages last year as there were divorces, or ex-pressed another way, the number of divorces last year was 50 percent of the num-ber of marriages. However, "divorce rate of 50 percent" makes it sound like half the married people get divorced each year, and this surface interpretation is wrong. Let's compare the number of divorces last year with the number of *total existing marriages* at the beginning of that year. This comparison gives a figure of about 1 percent. This means that last year, 1 percent of all existing marriages ended in di-vorce by the end of that year. Which is the correct divorce rate: 50 percent or 1 per-cent? They both are. The difference results from using different denominators. Both are legitimate, but they answer different questions. If the question is "What per-centage of existing marriages will end in divorce this year?" the answer is 1 percent. However, if the question is "What is the ratio of the number of marriages this year to the number of divorces this year?" the answer is 50 percent. If we don't examine a claim that the divorce rate is 50 percent, we might be led to believe that half of all existing marriages will end in divorce this year, which is extremely inaccurate.

See how percentages can be misleading? It is important that you always eval-uate numbers—especially percentages—to make sure you understand how they were computed. If you do not do this, you are in danger of assuming the wrong meaning, even when the figures are accurate. Sometimes you will not be able to find all the information you need in order to analyze a message; authors often do not provide enough detail. When detail is missing, you need to go to other mes-sages the author quotes (the author's primary sources) and conduct a focal plane analysis on those messages. You may be surprised to learn how often people take an accurate percentage from one message and use that percentage in a different context, where it is inaccurate.

Evaluation Trap 5: Misunderstanding Causal Relationships

Some arguments are based on *casual claims*. A causal claim is something like: A causes B, so when we have an A, a B will always follow; and when we have a B, there is always an A preceding it. It is natural for people to seek explanations for events they observe. However, sometimes people arrive at wrong explanations because of one or more *fallacies,* or errors in logic. One of these is the ecological fallacy, where an argument claims that there is a **causal relationship** between two things merely because they occur together. For example, in the 1950s it was found that crime rates were the highest in neighborhoods where immigrants were most numerous. Some people used this "co-occurrence" to argue that immigrants were a cause of crime. However, a careful examination of this situation reveals that immigrants were forced to live in neighborhoods where crime rates were already high; they could not afford more expensive housing in safer neighborhoods. Immigrants themselves committed very few of the crimes. Unless you examine this claim carefully, you would probably misinterpret the relationship.

Causal relationship
An inference that one element causes a reaction in another element.

Another error that can arise with a causal claim is the butterfly fallacy. This is named after the belief that if a butterfly flaps its wings today in the Amazon basin, it could trigger a chain of events that could eventually lead to rain in your hometown next week. The problem with this "connection" is that there are millions of simultaneous "causes" occurring at any moment. You would need to examine each link in the very long causal chain from the Amazon to your house in order to verify the claim that a butterfly actually caused the rain. In other words, be very careful with statements that jump from a particular cause to a far-removed effect.

Evaluation Trap 6: Misconstruing Comparative Claims

Be careful of **comparative claims**—ones that use relative words such as *better, larger, faster,* or *cheaper,* or *best, largest, fastest,* or *cheapest.* Examine them to see what is actually being compared. For example, many car commercials claim the advertised car has been rated best in its class. What is its "class"? Perhaps its class is defined in so narrow a way (e.g., cars weighing between 2500 and 2650 pounds, with a driver's side airbag only, and Sony radios as standard equipment) that it is the *only* car in its class.

Comparative claim
The judgment that one element is superior to another element in some way.

Evaluation Trap 7: Underdeveloped Abilities

As you work on developing your natural abilities, you will gain skill and confidence in solving problems. If your abilities are relatively weak, do not avoid using them; instead work on developing them, and they will get stronger. Using the tool of evaluation will become easier.

To conduct a good evaluation, you need to avoid impulsiveness, and you need to be able to think laterally. You also need the product of a good analysis, which relies on field independency and conceptual differentiation. With strong abilities, you will find it easier to be more careful, reasonable, diligent, and logical when making evaluative judgments.

Evaluation Trap 8: Underdeveloped Knowledge Structures

The more information you already have, the easier it is to make judgments about new information, as long as your existing knowledge structures contain accurate and useful information. When your knowledge structure includes only cognitive information, you have the basis for a logical reasoning process—but what happens when this logical process results in the need to make a moral or aesthetic judgment?

Such a limited knowledge structure can't help you accomplish that kind of task. For example, let's say you have a great deal of cognitive knowledge about the political process and the people and issues involved, but you don't have much information about moral systems. In this situation, you could not make a good evaluation about which position on an issue is the most ethical one, because you have no moral standard upon which to make such judgments well.

Don't be discouraged. Even if you have a relatively underdeveloped knowledge structure, this is better than an elaborate knowledge structure that is riddled with inaccurate and useless information. It is easier to start with a sketchy knowledge system and build it well than it is to go back through a huge existing knowledge structure and try to prune out all the bad information.

Evaluation Trap 9: Misunderstanding the Role of Emotions

An important part of evaluation is emotions. If you do not factor in how you feel about something, you may "over-intellectualize" your judgments and arrive at conclusions that are very logical but that just don't "feel right." You need to have enough awareness of your emotions to know where your preferences lie. Let your preferences influence your standards for evaluation. However, be careful that your preferences do not dominate the standards so that reason has no part in the evaluation.

Many evaluation decisions cannot be made well with the intellect alone. This is especially the case when you have multiple criteria and some elements meet the criteria while others do not. You are then faced with the problem of deciding which criteria are more important than others. To reach a summary judgment, you must make these decisions, and to do so, you need to factor in your emotions. However, this does not mean being frivolous and flighty—it means that you should try to draw on the emotional wisdom you've gained through past experiences. Try fantasizing about how you would feel if you had already made the evaluative decision one particular way. Do positive emotions arise? If so, you should probably go with that decision. Perhaps instead, this fantasizing makes you recall a bad decision you made in the past, and this memory triggers emotions you want to avoid. If so, you now know from your projected emotions that this might be a bad decision.

EXERCISE 5.1

PRACTICE AT EVALUATION

Try each of these exercises. If you get stuck, try to identify if you have fallen into a trap. Look back at the section on avoiding traps to try to get going again.

1. Make an assessment on the standard of cognitive utility.
   A. Begin with the elements you generated in the last exercise in the previous chapter, in which you analyzed a newspaper article on a controversy.
   B. Use your existing knowledge structure on the controversy as your standard for utility.

    C. Answer the following questions:
- 1. Which of the elements from the analysis would add *breadth* if incorporated into your existing knowledge structure on this controversy?
- 2. Which of the elements from the analysis would add *depth*?
- 3. Which of the elements from the analysis would add *weight*?

    D. Given your answers to the above three questions, which elements would have the highest utility? Which elements would have no utility?

2. Make an assessment on the standard of cognitive accuracy.
   A. Begin with the elements you generated in the last exercise in the previous chapter.
   B. Use your existing knowledge structure on the controversy as your standard for accuracy.
   C. Answer the following questions:
   - 1. Which elements meet your criterion for accuracy?
   - 2. How much confidence do you have in your standard for accuracy? That is, is it possible that what you regard as accurate facts in your existing knowledge structure may be faulty in some way?
   - 3. Where would you go (outside your existing knowledge structure) to find an external standard for judging the accuracy of the elements in this evaluation?

3. Make an assessment on an aesthetic standard.
   A. Rent a movie that was made from a book. Watch the movie and read the book. Analyze both along aesthetic dimensions. That is, who are the key characters and what are their major qualities? What are the key plot points? What is the theme?
   B. Use your knowledge structure about storytelling and write down your standard for a good movie. That is, what criteria should it have?
   C. Compare the elements in your analysis of the movie to your standard for a good movie. You will likely have multiple criteria—maybe some criteria for characters, other criteria for plot, and other criteria for theme.
   D. Make a summary judgment. On balance, do you judge this to be a good movie or not? Why?
   E. Compare the elements in your analysis of the book to your standard for a good book. Again, you will likely have multiple criteria.
   F. Make a summary judgment. On balance, do you judge this to be a good book or not? Why?
   G. Now the big aesthetic evaluation question: Was the movie or the book better? If you used the same standards of storytelling for the book and the movie, then this is a relatively easy question to answer. But if you used a different set of standards for a book and a movie, then you will need to "compare apples and oranges" so to speak, but this can be done if you think carefully through all the steps above to arrive at a summary judgment.

4. Make an assessment on an emotional standard.
   A. Use the elements from your analysis of the movie and the book.
   B. What kind of emotions did you expect to get from this story? How strong did you expect those emotions to be?
   C. Compare your expectations to the emotions you actually felt. Did your emotions exceed or fall short of your expectations?
   D. If you experienced strong emotions, what did the author of the book do to trigger such strong emotions? What did the director of the movie do that evoked such strong emotions?
   E. If you did not experience strong emotions, what could the author of the book have done differently to evoke stronger emotions? What could the director of the movie have done differently to evoke stronger emotions?
   F. On balance, do you think the director of the movie or the author of the book is more skilled at evoking emotions? To what extent do you think this difference is traceable to raw ability and to what extent is it attributable to the difference between books and movies?

5. Make an assessment on a moral standard.
   A. Use the elements from your analysis of the movie and the book.
   B. Sort through the elements from your analysis and find the plot points where a character was faced with a moral choice.
   C. Write down your moral standard for such actions. Is your moral standard an absolute one? If so, then it should be fairly easy to make the judgment about whether a character in a situation met your moral standard for behavior or fell below it. However, if your moral standard is not absolute—that is, it depends on the situation—then your judgment process will be more complicated as you consider the elements in this particular situation.

CONCLUSION

If you encounter a message without evaluating it, you allow it to pass into your knowledge structures unexamined. As a result, faulty and useless information gets cataloged along with accurate and important information. It is therefore important to judge new information against some standard. A good standard is one that you select after considering all the options, including cognitive, moral, emotional, and aesthetic components. The standard should have clear criteria to guide your judgments on the elements.

The five-step algorithm presented in this chapter is a general formula for conducting evaluations. However, many evaluation tasks are partially specified, and this means that the formula will have gaps. You learned two heuristics to help you think about how to bridge two frequently occurring gaps: constructing categories and making a summary judgment when dealing with multiple criteria. Finally, you read about nine traps that can prevent you from completing good evaluations. Knowing about these traps ahead of time can help you avoid them and stay focused on the task of evaluating message elements by systematically comparing them to standards.

Skill 3: Induction

LEARNING OBJECTIVES

By reading this chapter, you will:

1. Learn how to develop your skill of induction.
2. Understand how to use two types of heuristics to help you with the skill of evaluation.
   - Power of falsification
   - Adapt to tentativeness
3. Understand how to avoid five traps that can prevent you from using the skill of induction well.
   - Getting lost in the details
   - Reluctance to use intuition
   - Generalizing too far
   - Narrow base of observations
   - Faulty base for generalizing

Pattern

Commonalities across elements.

Generalizing

Making a claim that a pattern you infer from observing a small number of elements is the same pattern you would find if you examined all the elements in a set.

We use induction when we make broad statements about things after observing only a few examples. Let's say you watch a movie where a young child throws a temper tantrum. Then later you are in a store and see a young child whining because his father won't buy him some candy. You find yourself thinking: "All children are so spoiled these days!" After experiencing two examples of bad behavior in children, you have inferred a **pattern** (both children were spoiled) and generalized that pattern to all children. In essence, induction is the skill of inferring a pattern among a few observations, and then **generalizing** that pattern.

All of us want a good amount of useful knowledge about how the world works, but we cannot possibly experience everything the world has to offer. Our experience is always limited. No matter how many people we meet, we will never be able to meet everyone; and yet, we want to feel that we understand broad patterns of human behavior.

Induction allows us to expand from our limited experience and get a sense of the world in general. With the skill of induction, we can use our limited experience to construct an understanding about things beyond our particular experiences. We use induction to move from our limited contact with a few examples of something to generalize about *all* examples of that something.

Induction is the skill that underlies the scientific method. With the scientific method, you first pose a question, then make observations, formulate a hypothesis, test the hypothesis with more observations, and draw conclusions; if the hypothesis is supported, you generalize. Psychologists often refer to people as "naive scientists" because of the way they approach problem solving in their everyday lives. The word "scientists" refers to the use of the scientific method or induction, and the word "naive" refers to the lack of knowledge about the full power of induction as well as its limitations.

Efficiency

Using a skill with as little effort as possible.

Accuracy

Using a skill to arrive at conclusions supported by observations, free of false inferences and conclusions.

Of course, when you confront most of your everyday problems and challenges, you do not need to know the full power of induction or be concerned about its limitations. In everyday life, you are probably motivated by **efficiency**—you want to arrive at a solution as quickly as possible, then move on to other things. The consequences of being wrong are usually slight. In other situations, such as college courses, you need to be motivated more by accuracy. In school, being right is more important than speed alone. When you are guided by the goal of **accuracy**, you need to know more about the process of induction and how to get the most out of it. You need to be more systematic in using this skill and avoid traps that could lead you to inaccurate conclusions. In the example about children, if you had made more observations and constructed the inference more carefully, the resulting generalization would have been a more accurate reflection of the nature of young children. You would have found that most children do behave badly from time to time, but only under certain conditions. Most of the time and in most conditions, children do not behave badly. In this example, the *pattern was inferred* accurately (both children were spoiled), but the *generalization* was inaccurate (not all children are spoiled).

You already know how to use the skill of induction to achieve efficiency. The information in this chapter will help you develop your induction skill to achieve accuracy. In your everyday life, where inferences are often not very important, you will still try to achieve efficiency and therefore use induction in an informal way. However, in situations where your inferences need to be more accurate (such as important course assignments that will be graded), you will need to forgo efficiency and switch to accuracy as a goal. This will require a more formal application of induction.

To do induction well, you need: (a) the ability to recognize a pattern in the particulars, (b) confidence in the set of particulars as being able to represent some larger group (of people, places, time periods, or situations), and (c) the willingness to make the leap to a general statement.

THE INDUCTION ALGORITHM

Induction is a process of formulating a question, making observations, inferring a pattern, generalizing the pattern, and testing your claim. Remember that you live in an information-saturated society, where you are continually making observations; you cannot avoid doing so. Therefore, the inductive process does not start when you make observations (which is all the time). Instead, the inductive process really starts when something grabs your attention in a way that stimulates you to begin asking questions.

Step 1: Formulate a Question

The process of induction begins when some kind of a question occurs to you about things you observe. For example, suppose you are taking a college course and find it very difficult. This can trigger all kinds of questions. You might begin to wonder if all courses in that academic department are difficult. If so, maybe you feel you don't have an aptitude for that subject matter. You might wonder if it is just your professor who is difficult—maybe the other courses in that department will not be as demanding. Or perhaps it is not the professor but the amount of reading that is difficult. Each of these concerns can be expressed as a question.

The Skill of Induction

Purpose: To infer patterns across individual observations
Process:

1. Formulate a question.
2. Observe several messages of a given type.
3. Infer a pattern: Look for commonalities across those messages.
4. Generalize the pattern: Claim that the commonalities are present in all messages of the given type.
5. To continue to test your claim, examine additional messages of that type to determine if the same characteristics are present.

Sometimes your question is more fully formed. For example, let's say you watch a local television newscast and notice that the first few stories deal with crime and violence that make you feel fearful. You also notice that as the newscast continues, the stories deal with weather, sports, and features where the newscasters joke around and make you feel silly and happy. It strikes you that there seems to be a pattern. You wonder if *all* newscasts begin by hooking viewers with fear, and then proceed to make them feel happy with humorous or uplifting stories.

Step 2: Make More Observations

Your question sets up a need to make some observations. The question also directs your attention to certain elements in the observations you plan to make. In the newscast example, the question guides you to watch more newscasts and pay attention to the *types* of stories and how they may change in tone during the newscast.

The types of observations you need to make are guided by your question. If a difficult course is bothering you, several questions are possible, and the focus of the observations changes depending on the question. For example, let's say you express your question as: *Are all courses in this academic department difficult?* With this as your question, you would have to take more courses in that department, or at least talk to other students who have. Suppose instead you formulated the question: *Is the professor the reason for my difficulty in the course?* In that case, you would need to take more courses from this professor, or at least make more observations about her or him. Or the question could be: *Is it the amount of reading that is difficult?* To answer this question, you would make additional observations by asking other students if they find the amount of reading to be too much. The way you formulate the question guides the way you select additional observations. The more clearly you express the question, the better you will be able to determine what observations to make.

The first two steps of induction can be repeated. You might want to do this when it is difficult to formulate a clear question right away. Perhaps at the beginning you don't have a clear question but only a nagging feeling. It may take several cycles of steps 1 and 2 to progress from the nagging feeling to the statement of a clear question.

For example, suppose you have a nagging feeling that something is not right in a course. You could begin by asking: *Is the workload the problem?* You think about other courses you have taken, and you ask other students in the course about workload. They tell you the workload in this course is about average, and when you think back on your other courses you agree that the workload is not excessive. The question about workload leads nowhere, so you need to find another line of questioning. You might ask: *Is the problem the subject matter taught in this department?* If it is your first course in the department and you have no personal experience with this particular area, you would need to ask other students who have taken courses in this department before. Let's say they tell you the material is not particularly difficult—certainly not as difficult as the subject matter taught in some other departments. This line of questioning about subject matter also leads nowhere. You must come up with yet another line of questioning to guide your further observations. The cycle of steps 1 and 2 continues until you feel you are "on the right track"—you have a question that is going to lead you to make the kinds of observations that will explain your nagging feeling.

To finish up this example, let's say that you finally ask the question: *Is it me?* You might wonder if you don't have a natural talent in the subject matter while many other students do. If this line of questioning seems to be promising, then you could refine your question to be something like: *Where do my natural talents lie?* The search for the answer to this question would lead you to think about courses in other departments, where the subject matter, course experiences, and testing are very different from the course that is bothering you. By continuing to ask questions and let each one guide your observations, you should come closer and closer to finding the pattern of your natural talents and matching them to patterns of requirements in different types of courses.

Step 3: Infer a Pattern

When you have a clear question and are making observations, now you need to look for commonalities across those observations. This requires a careful examination of the elements you are observing.

Let's return to the newscast example. With each newscast, you need to do a component analysis to identify a list of the stories. Then, ask yourself if the same pattern of stories occurs in each newscast. Are the fear stories presented first, then the humorous and human interest stories? Once this pattern occurs to you, you can look at the sequence of stories in other newscasts to see if your guess at a pattern holds up.

Let's say you watch a second newscast and perceive the same feelings of fear at the beginning and feelings of happiness at the end. You then watch a third, then a fourth newscast. In each newscast you see the same pattern. At this point in the inductive process, you have inferred a pattern, which is: *The initial stories evoke fear, then the later stories evoke happiness.*

The process of inferring a pattern requires trial and error. You make some observations and notice some things that happen over and over. Write them down. This list of commonalities is your initial pattern. Then observe more examples and see which items on the list apply to the new observations. If any do not, delete them. Repeat this process over and over until you have a list of things that are true of every observation you make.

This list is an *inference*—a pattern that you have observed. It is saying that you've noticed commonalities in the specific elements you have observed. If you observed four newscasts, the inference is only about those four newscasts. At this point, you are not claiming that a fifth or sixth newscast would have the same pattern.

Step 4: Generalize the Pattern

The next step is to generalize the pattern. To do this, you claim that the pattern you inferred from your limited number of observations is not limited to *only* those observations, but that it is more general. You claim that the inference will be true of all possible observations.

You inferred a pattern across the four newscasts. However, you are really trying to learn something about newscasts in general, not just those four. If you generalize the pattern to all newscasts, you have a more interesting claim: *All newscasts begin with stories of crime and violence to evoke fear in the audience, then they shift to stories that will make the audience feel happy.* This **general claim** lets you feel you know something about all newscasts, without having to observe them all. You have arrived at an inference about all newscasts even though you only expended the effort to observe four.

When we generalize, we are removing the limitations of time, space, situation, or people. You removed the limitation of time by moving beyond four newscasts (about two hours of airtime) to *all* newscasts. The general claim is not limited to four newscasts, or one week of newscasts, or newscasts only in the evening, or newscasts only during sweeps months, or newscasts only during one season of the year, or newscasts only this year. This statement is also very general as far as space—that is, it is not limited to newscasts in only one television market. Our generalization implies that the pattern holds in all 215 local markets in the United States; it also does not limit itself to only U. S. local broadcast markets. It is also very general as far as people—that is, it is not limited to only stories presented by people of one gender, age grouping, or ethnic background.

General claim

Argument that the pattern found in the elements you observed extends to a larger class of elements you have not observed.

Step 5: Continue to Test Your General Claim

To test the general claim, you need to examine more messages to see if it holds. To do this efficiently, consider the dimensions that make your statement general—time, space, situation, and people. Select your messages strategically in those areas so as to maximize the return on your effort.

As you continue to gather observations, you will probably find ones that contradict the general claim. When that happens, you will revise the general claim to make it narrow. The more testing you do, the more precisely you can craft the generalization and the more confidence you can have in its accuracy. This testing step is what separates a good process of generalization from a poor one.

In everyday life, we frequently skip this step. When we are in a hurry or when accuracy is not very important, we do not continue to observe examples to see if the generalization holds. As a result, many of our generalizations are wrong. If your goal with induction is accuracy, then it is important to continue testing your general claims. Even if you are very insightful in seeing patterns across as few as two messages, there is no guarantee that the pattern will hold in the third or 503rd observation. So the more observations you have to support your claim, the more credible your claim will be. How many observations are required? There is no way to give a general answer to this question. For some guidelines on this point, see the falsification heuristic below.

HEURISTICS

Of all of the thinking skills, the tool of induction is least likely to be used with fully specified problems. This is because fully specified problems give you all the information you need—there is no need to make an inference, because you already know everything you need to solve the problem. Hence heuristics are especially important with the skill of induction. Generalizations can never be proven completely—to do that, you would have to observe every single item you are generalizing about. You may be asking: But if we can never prove a general claim, how can we ever know if the claim is accurate? The answer is to think less about accuracy and more about *confidence*. Although you can never prove the accuracy of a general claim, you can increase your level of confidence in it. How can you increase your level of confidence? By using heuristics. This section presents two heuristics to help you increase your confidence in general claims.

Induction Heuristic 1: Power of Falsification

You will never have absolute certainty that your claim is accurate, because you cannot examine all of the examples. If you did examine them all, you would no longer be making a general claim; you would simply be stating an observed pattern. In practice, often this is simply not possible. Sheer numbers frequently prevent it. If your generalization is not limited by time, then it covers examples from the past, and those may not be available for observation.

Even though you can never completely confirm the *accuracy* of a generalization, you can discover *inaccuracies*. Thus, although proving a generalization is completely accurate is impossible, proving it is *inaccurate* is relatively easy. All you need is one element that does not fit the pattern to prove that the pattern does not always hold. When you have found a misfit, you have falsified the pattern.

The purpose of **falsification** is not to negate a pattern completely—that would be counterproductive, invalidating all the work you did to develop the general claim. Instead, the power in falsification is its ability to define the boundaries of the pattern. Falsification shows you where to alter the pattern so that it more accurately reflects the elements. Returning to the example about newscasts, let's say that you viewed 900 newscasts and found that every one of them fit the pattern—then you view one that does *not* fit that pattern. Does this mean you have falsified the entire pattern and you must throw out all your work and start over? Of course not. Instead, you have reached the boundary of the pattern. Your task now is to examine the characteristics of the "misfit" newscast to see how it differs from the other 900 newscasts. Perhaps the 900 newscasts were all from U. S. television stations, and the one that did not fit the pattern was from a Canadian station. In this case, you have found the limit to the pattern and must revise the generalization. But before you do, it would be good to examine newscasts from other Canadian stations and also perhaps stations in Mexico and other countries. Depending on what you find, you might revise the pattern from "all television stations" to only "U. S. television stations."

Use the power of falsification to find the boundaries of your claim. Think about what the limits might be in terms of time, place, situation, and people. Observe elements that test these limits. When you find examples that do not fit the pattern, then you have found a boundary. If you examine instances where you thought your claim might not hold, yet it still does hold, then you have reason to expand the boundaries. Thus, testing your claim for a variety of times, places,

Falsification

Finding evidence counter to your inferred pattern.

situations, and people is better than testing in a narrow range. When you observe within a narrow range, even if you do find support for the claim, this does not help you delineate its boundaries.

With falsification, your goal here is *not* to try to prove your general claim; you can never do that, because you can't possibly make all the observations you would need to show that there are no exceptions. Instead your goal should be to find the outer limits of your claim, by discovering where the statement no longer holds. In the newscast example, you generalized to include all television newscasts, then reduced the claim to all television newscasts in the United States. Let's try to find another boundary. Suppose your observations had all been on *local* newscasts up until this point; now you want to check for patterns in *national* newscasts. You watch some national newscasts and find inconsistencies with the general claim. You have found another limit to your general claim, and you must reword it accordingly. It would now read: *All* **local** *newscasts* **in the United States** *begin with stories of crime and violence to evoke fear in the audience, then they shift to stories that will make the audience feel happy.* This is still a general claim covering thousands of examples that you never observed, but it is not as general as the original general claim. By testing, you have lost some breadth, but gained much accuracy.

By revealing areas of inaccuracy, the testing and falsification process allows you to improve generalizations. This is very important, because it reduces the number of false generalizations in your knowledge structures and thus improves your level of confidence in the general claims you make.

Induction Heuristic 2: Adapt to Tentativeness

Tentativeness

Belief that your inferred pattern may be falsified later; an attitude you must hold while doing induction.

Remember that you can never fully confirm any inferred statement of a general pattern. Statements are always **tentative.** That is something with which you must get comfortable.

Some people feel very uneasy when they are told that the patterns they infer might be wrong and the claims they generalize might be too broad. They don't like being vulnerable to criticisms like these. However, they can take comfort in the fact that this kind of criticism is a two-way street. People who criticize your patterns or generalizations must back up their criticism with evidence of exceptions to the pattern. If they cannot do this, then their criticism is groundless. If instead they can provide evidence that the pattern is limited, then you have benefitted by those observations and learned something. Remember, the ultimate goal of education is not to avoid negative things such as ignorance and criticism. Those things are part of life. The goal of education is to try to turn these negative things into tools that will help you understand the world better. Turn ignorance into curiosity and criticism into questioning.

While no general claim can ever be fully supported, there are, however, various degrees of support. Just saying that all statements are tentative does not mean that they are all equally valuable or accurate. Some have more support. While there is no such thing as *total* support, there is a difference between a haphazardly inferred statement based on only two observations and a carefully inferred statement based on 20.

AVOIDING TRAPS

nduction is almost always used with partially specified problems, so there are many traps that can prevent you from arriving at an accurate and useful solution. This section provides warnings about five major traps. The first two deal with problems that might keep you from noticing patterns. The other three traps deal with generalizing those patterns.

Induction Trap 1: Getting Lost in the Details

Sometimes people get so wrapped up in all the details in each message that they miss seeing the big picture. This happens less with field independent people, but even those people may sometimes feel overwhelmed by the details. When this happens, you need to realize you are too close to the task. Take a break, then come back later with a different perspective that will allow you to see the big picture, which is, in essence, the pattern.

Induction Trap 2: Reluctance to Use Intuition

Induction requires the use of some **intuition,** especially in the early stages when you need to find a pattern in the elements in a set. By "intuition" I do not mean taking a wild guess, which is the way many people define intuition in everyday language. Instead, I use the definition found in most dictionaries, where intuition is defined as the direct perception of truths without any reasoning process. Intuition is when you look at the set of elements and simply "see" the pattern without going through any reasoning process at all. It is as if a light bulb is turned on in your head and you "see" things much more clearly.

Intuition
Direct perception of patterns independent of any reasoning process; insightful learning.

This is not to say that reasoning and logic are not important in the inductive process. They are important, but they are most useful *after* a pattern occurs to you. At that point you need to think logically about how to make more observations to test the pattern you came up with. Thus the inductive process values "jumping to a conclusion" early on, but that is not the end of the process. The conclusion (pattern) needs to be tested with more observations.

Although some people think of intuition as unscientific, unsystematic, and unsupported, it is essential to the inductive process. If you fear taking the leap of inference to state a pattern, you will be stuck in a trap. Take a chance and make a guess. Even if it is wrong, you will have the direction to make additional observations. If you find evidence of that pattern, your guess was good, so keep making observations. If you do not find evidence of that pattern, then ask yourself: What is missing? Looking for answers to that question will help you find different patterns.

Induction Trap 3: Generalizing Too Far

Generalizing means making a claim that the pattern you perceive in the few observations you made also holds for a much larger set of elements, which you did not observe. You might be wondering "How far can I go? How broad can my general claim be?" This is a good question, but do not expect a quantitative answer to it. Instead, the answer is in terms of *levels*. The examples you observe are limited by time, situation, and people. Each of these concepts has levels. As you move up each level, you are including a larger class of things. For example, think about moving up levels of people. Let's say you visit your friend Sara in her hometown of Savannah, Georgia. When you meet several of her friends, you observe that those people are very sociable and friendly. So you conclude that Sara's hometown friends are all very sociable and friendly. You have not met all of Sara's hometown friends; you have only met a few, but on the basis of those few observations you have generalized to a class of people (all of Sara's hometown friends). Let's call this a Level 1 generalization, because you have observed a pattern in a *few* of Sara's friends and moved up one level to *all* of Sara's friends. A Level 2 generalization would be to say that *all people* in Savannah are sociable and friendly. This would include all of Sara's hometown friends plus many more people. A Level 3 generalization would be that all people in Georgia are sociable and friendly. This would also include all the people in Savannah, which includes all of Sara's hometown friends.

How many levels should you generalize? It is safest to move up only one level. To generalize to one higher level is easier for people to accept and for you to defend than generalizing up several levels. Going up a second level opens you to criticism like: "How do you know all people in Savannah are sociable and friendly when you have only met a few of Sara's hometown friends? What about people Sara does not know—how do you know that they are sociable and friendly?" This is a valid point. How *do* you know? You have no evidence. So it is better to gather at least some evidence to represent that level of people. Generalize up one level at a time, and gather evidence at that more general level to support that claim. Then move up one more level and gather evidence at that level, and so forth.

The more you generalize, the shakier will be the ground on which you defend your generalizations. To illustrate this, let's say that during your visit with Sara, you met four of her friends. She has 12 friends in all, so your generalization about all her friends is based on observing one-third of her friends. Now let's say you make six more observations, noticing that servers in restaurants, clerks in stores, and people on the street are also very sociable and friendly. From these 10 observations (four of Sara's friends and six around town), you conclude that all people in Savannah, Georgia, are sociable and friendly. This group of people is much larger, about half a million people.

Now, let's say you take some day trips and visit some tourist spots around Georgia. During those trips you notice from 20 observations that people are sociable and friendly. So you conclude that all people in Georgia are sociable and friendly. This group of people includes all people in Savannah, which also includes all Sara's friends. You have now moved up to an even higher level, which includes many more people, perhaps 5 million. Every time you go up a level, the ratio of the number of observations to the number of people in the group goes down—way down. So while your generalizations are still based on some evidence, the proportion of that evidence to the size of the total group is becoming very small indeed.

With induction, you end up walking a very thin line with a big trap on either side of you. On one side is the trap of overgeneralizing, where your conclusion looks like wild speculation that you cannot possibly defend when challenged. The only thing you can do to avoid this trap is to make as many observations as possible and make sure they are not clustered too much in one level (with only one type of person, one type of situation, or one time). On the other side of the line is the trap of refusing to generalize at all. This trap dooms you to treat every observation as unique and not part of a larger pattern. You then are in danger of losing sight of the big picture, because *the big picture is a pattern.* There *are* patterns across people, ideas, and events. Recognizing these patterns can help you understand the nature of things, predict what will happen, and explain where you fit in the larger world.

Induction Trap 4: Narrow Base of Observations

Sometimes people generalize from a very small set of observations—sometimes from only one. In this trap, people focus on an isolated incident and conclude that it represents them all. For example, you might read a news story about a criminal who copied an unusual bank robbery from a movie, and conclude that movies are responsible for the high rate of crime in society. Concluding that *all* movies are bad because *one person* copies a particular action in *one movie* is a faulty induction. No one movie can represent the incredible variety of all movies. Also, concluding that movies alone are responsible for crime in society is a faulty induction, because this conclusion fails to include the many factors that can lead a person to commit a crime.

We often fall into this induction trap when we assess risk in our personal lives. Often the media will present a story—either in news or a drama—of an airplane mishap, a stalker, or something else that makes us fearful. From this one portrayal, we tend to overestimate the risk to *ourselves* from this type of threat—while ignoring other things (that the media do not talk about) that may pose a much higher risk. For example, in 1987 many news reports told about the risk to children from asbestos in older school buildings. Fear spread as people inferred that *all* schools had problems and that their children were at risk. Almost overnight the asbestos-removal industry more than doubled its revenue. However, the actual risk of a premature death from exposure to asbestos is 1 in 100,000. Compare this to the rate of premature death due to being struck by lightning, which is 3 in 100,000.

Many people believe that exposure to X-rays in dentists' and doctors' offices is risky. It does present a small risk—but the risk of premature death due to smoking cigarettes is 2,920 *times* that of premature death due to exposure to diagnostic X-rays (Mathews, 1992). However, many people calmly accept the risk of smoking but feel endangered when a dentist X-rays their teeth once a year.

Induction Trap 5: Faulty Base for Generalizing

Another trap is observing a pattern in one kind of message, then generalizing to not just a larger set of messages of that kind, but to a different kind of message altogether. For example, sometimes people want to find a general principle for making relationships work. Rather than observing relationships in the real world, they will watch relationships among characters in television programs. When they see a pattern in those television relationships, they generalize that pattern to the real world. This is faulty, because they have not observed relationships in the real world and therefore do not have the correct base of observations to generalize from.

EXERCISE 6.1

PRACTICE AT INDUCTION

1. Pick a textbook for one of your courses. Flip through it to see if there are pictures. Your question is: Do my textbooks have pictures? (This is a focal analysis.)

   Choose another textbook and see if it contains pictures. Keep making observations in many different kinds of textbooks.

   After examining about half a dozen texts, do you see a pattern developing? Do all textbooks have pictures? If not, what types of textbooks have pictures? That is:
   - Are texts in introductory courses more likely to have pictures?
   - Are texts used in certain academic departments more likely to have pictures?
   - Do texts that cost more tend to have pictures, or not?

   Keep looking at texts to see if your claim holds up. Look for examples to falsify your claim.

2. Think of the movies you like best. Go through your memory and list those movies.

   Analyze these movies for elements that you particularly liked. Do the same kinds of elements show up in all the movies you like? If so, write a general statement that expresses what you like best in movies.

   Now continue to test this general statement. Think of television shows you like. Does that statement apply to TV shows? If so, expand the statement to apply to TV programs as well as movies.

   Continue to test your general statement. Think of novels you have read and liked the most. Does the statement also apply to print stories? If so, expand it to apply to print stories.

   Now think of happenings in your real life that you have enjoyed the most. Does the statement apply to what happens to you in real life? If so, expand it to apply to all events—mediated stories as well as real-world happenings.

   Think back on the pattern of expanding the statement. How far were you willing to go with it? If you could not expand it past movies, why? What is it about movies that makes certain stories your favorite when they are on the big screen but not when they are on TV?

3. Think about the people whom you regard as your closest friends.

   Analyze those friendships for elements that you particularly like. Do those same kinds of elements show up in all your friendships? If so, write a general statement that expresses what you value most in close friendships.

   Continue to test this general statement. Think of professors you like. Does the statement apply to them too? If so, expand it.

   Now think of your relatives whom you especially like. Does the general statement also apply to them? If so, expand it. Continue to test and expand the general statement to explore what you value in people.

CONCLUSION

The process of induction begins with observations of a set of elements. You need to use intuition to perceive patterns in those elements. Once you have found a tentative pattern, continue observing to make sure the pattern appears consistently. Finally, generalize by claiming that the pattern also holds in a much larger class of elements that you did not observe.

Inferred patterns should always be regarded as tentative explanations. Someone could always come along later and find an example that does not fit the pattern. Such "misfit" examples are valuable, because they allow you to reformulate the pattern or clarify its limits.

Several heuristics provide guidelines for good induction. These heuristics can help you use the power of falsification and adapt to tentativeness. Finally, it is important to avoid traps, particularly getting lost in details, being reluctant to use intuition, generalizing too far, using too narrow a base of observations, and relying on a faulty base for generalizing.

CHAPTER 7

Skill 4: Deduction

LEARNING OBJECTIVES

By reading this chapter, you will:

1. Learn how to develop your skill of deduction.
2. Understand how to avoid four traps that can prevent you from using the skill of deduction well.
   - Faulty major premise
   - Fact vs. belief as a premise
   - Irrelevant major premise
   - Too simple a major premise
3. Understand how to use four types of heuristics to help you with the skill of deduction.
   - Probability premise
   - Conditional reasoning
   - Try to be rational
   - Build knowledge structures

Syllogism

A set of three statements in which a conclusion is reasoned from two beginning premises.

Major premise

A general principle or rule.

Minor premise

An observation of a particular.

Deduction is the skill of using a few premises to reason logically toward a conclusion. The basic process of deduction follows the form of a **syllogism**. A syllogism is a set of three statements. The first statement, called the **major premise**, is usually a general principle or rule. The second statement, called the **minor premise**, is usually an observation. The third statement is the conclusion that follows from the first two statements.

Here is the classic example of a syllogism:

All men are mortal. (major premise)
Socrates is a man. (minor premise)
Socrates is mortal. (conclusion)

The major premise states a general proposition. The minor premise provides information about something specific (in this case a specific person) in a way that relates it to the major premise. The observation in the second premise fits the rule in the first premise, and we conclude that Socrates is mortal.

Deduction is the skill that the fictional detective Sherlock Holmes employed so successfully to interpret clues and solve crimes. He knew a great deal about the physical world and about human behavior. He knew how to select general principles (major premises) from his knowledge structures. He had keen powers of observation, so he knew what clues were the most relevant (minor premises). When he observed a clue (such as a scratch on a lock, mud on someone's shoes, or the gardener taking walks in the middle of the night), he set up a process of reasoning where he considered the clue in conjunction with a major premise, and he deduced a conclusion.

You already use this skill in your everyday life, although you may not refer to it as "deduction." For example, you probably have a general principle such as: *Working hard in a course leads to a high grade.* Also, you probably monitor your own study behavior and make observations such as, *I have worked hard in this course.* With these major and minor premises, you are likely to conclude with confidence that: *I will earn a high grade in this course.*

At this point you might be thinking: "This is so obvious!" That is precisely the point—deduction should be obvious. The essence of deduction is to reduce things to a simple logical process where the conclusion seems so obvious that no one would dispute it. Let's take a look at the algorithm that will help you do this.

The Skill of Deduction

Purpose: To use general principles to construct a conclusion about an example
Process:
1. Begin with an observation.
2. Identify a relevant general principle.
3. Use the two premises and reason to a conclusion.

THE DEDUCTION ALGORITHM

Step 1: Begin with an Observation

You have probably heard the phrase "Don't make the same mistake twice." In the literal sense, it is impossible to make exactly the same mistake twice, because situations change and people change; you can never have the exact same experience twice. In a more profound sense, the phrase tells you to learn from your mistakes. The way to learn is to get beyond the details of a particular mistake and look for a general principle, so that the next time the same type of situation occurs, you can act differently.

Or, you see something happen in your everyday life and wonder why. You are less interested in the particular observation for itself than in what it means in the broader picture—you want to learn something that you can apply to other instances.

Suppose you get back your first essay test in a particular course and are shocked to see that you did poorly. You could look at how your answer on each question was graded, but that is likely to give you information at too specific a level. You might find that on one question you earned few points because you did not provide much evidence to back up your argument. On another question perhaps you lost points because a definition was missing a key element. But what you really want to know is not what you did wrong on individual answers, but why you performed poorly on the test overall.

Working on the details of the past test will do nothing by itself to help you improve your grade in the course. Instead, you need to shift your attention to the future. What if you could use what you learned about how to craft answers to essay test questions on the next test? That would help you improve your overall grade in the course. In order to do this, you need to find some general principle about test taking that could help you avoid making mistakes on the next exam.

Step 2: Identify a Relevant General Principle

In this step, you search your knowledge structures to find a principle that can help you interpret the observation. This is one reason why knowledge structures are so important. If you don't have many useful knowledge structures, then you will not have many general principles to help you understand your experiences in everyday life. For example, people who have highly developed knowledge structures about communication and psychology will be better able to understand their relationships. People who have highly developed knowledge structures about economics and business will be better able to understand investments and plan for their financial futures.

How do these principles get into your knowledge structures? They come from education. In fact, the primary purpose of education is to give you general principles, or at least the means to find them or construct them yourself. By education I mean both formal education (in school) and informal education (self-motivated and self-guided learning).

In formal education, your courses expose you to a wide variety of ideas. That is why high schools usually require students to study literature, history, physical science, math, and a foreign language. Most colleges require freshmen and sophomores to take "general education"—courses distributed across the major bodies of knowledge—so that you experience a broad **liberal education.**

Liberal education

Acquisition of general principles and the skills to use them well.

The product of a good liberal education is not knowing a huge number of facts. Instead, its value is that you learn a set of well-organized general principles (knowledge structures) that you can apply deductively in almost any area of experience. Such a set of general principles gives you enormous power to explain a wide range of thoughts, experiences, and behaviors.

Step 3: Use the Two Premises to Reason Logically to a Conclusion

The third step is to use the premises from the two previous steps to reach a conclusion through logical reasoning. There are two forms of logical reasoning: classification and linear reasoning. Which one you choose depends on how the two premises relate.

The Socrates example is a *categorical* syllogism: it is about whether Socrates belongs in a certain category. The category is "mortal," and the rule is that all men are mortal. So when we observe a particular man and wonder whether to put him in the category of "mortal" or "immortal," the rule (general principle) says we must put him in the "mortal" category. This form of reasoning is classification.

Let's return to the example about the essay test. This too requires classification. You observe that you did poorly on an exam. You search your experience and locate the general principle: *If I do not study enough, I will do poorly on an exam.* Applying that rule along with your observation, you logically conclude that you did not study enough.

In contrast to classification reasoning, there is also *linear reasoning.* Linear reasoning also starts with two premises and reasons to a third, but neither of the premises is major or minor, general or particular. Instead both premises operate at the same level of importance or generality. That is, they are both general principles, or they are both observations.

The key to linear reasoning is to focus on associations between the two premises. Consider the following example:

Moe is smarter than Larry.
Larry is smarter than Curly.

Who is the smartest of the three? The answer, of course, is Moe. This conclusion is easy to reach when the two premises are stated clearly and in parallel form.

When the two premises are not stated in parallel form—such as when one is positive and one is negative—the reasoning process takes more effort. To illustrate:

Sally is not as smart as Ellen.
Sally is smarter than Harry.

Who is the smartest? The answer is Ellen, but this requires a bit more mental effort to reason out. Let's try one more example.

Professor Alplanap is a harder grader than Professor Bootreau.
Professor Cawleeni is an easier grader than Professor Bootreau.

When we compare the three professors, we conclude that Professor Alplanap grades the hardest.

Up to this point in the chapter, the process of deduction has been simplified so you can understand its essence and become comfortable with it. The remaining two sections of this chapter examine some of the typical challenges of deduction. The next section, on traps, examines most significant challenges, which lie in selecting the premises. Heuristics follow that will help guide you through the reasoning process once you have your premises. Notice that this chapter, unlike the previous three, deals with traps before heuristics. This is because deduction appears so simple, and its algorithm makes it seem that deductive problems are fully specified, so you may think there is no need for heuristics. But deduction presents some serious traps. Once you appreciate the nature of these traps, you will better understand the need for heuristics.

AVOIDING TRAPS

You might wonder what the big deal is—why do we need an entire chapter on something so simple and logical? But the simplicity is deceptive. When Sherlock Holmes was asked how he solved what appeared to be a complicated mystery, he would say, "It was elementary!" meaning it was simple. Yes, the reasoning process *was* simple, but identifying which observations (clues) should be minor premises and deciding which general principle should be the major premise was more difficult. This is always the challenge with deduction. Once you are confident that you have identified the right minor premise and major premise, reasoning to a conclusion *is* usually elementary.

Setting up a clear pair of statements that lets you apply classification or linear reasoning to arrive at a clear conclusion can be difficult. The world rarely presents such neat problems. Instead, problems are typically partially specified. You must select which observations to use for your minor premise and search for your own general principles to use for the major premises.

Because human thinking is so varied and complex, there is no way to list all the possible traps. This section covers three traps related to the major premise. This is the starting place for the reasoning process. If the starting place is faulty, irrelevant, or oversimplified, then the reasoning process will not lead to a useful conclusion. Keep in mind that many other traps exist, and be vigilant for them.

Deduction Trap 1: Faulty Major Premise

Deduction must begin with a major premise that is accurate. In the Socrates syllogism, if we began with the premise "All men live forever" instead of "All men are mortal," then we would have:

All men live forever.
Socrates is a man.
Therefore Socrates will live forever.

Faulty major premise
When the general principle in a syllogism is wrong.

When a deductive process begins with a faulty premise, it will arrive at a false conclusion, even though the reasoning process is logical. The example above is a very clear case of a **faulty major premise,** but in everyday life, it is not always clear when the major premise is faulty. Some major premises are widely accepted, but wide acceptance does not ensure its accuracy. For example, there was a time when it was widely accepted that the earth was flat. Many principles that are widely accepted today will be found to be faulty, and future generations will look back on some of our accepted principles and wonder what we were thinking.

The trap is blindly accepting principles and not examining them. You may have incorporated wrong information into your knowledge structures, resulting in a faulty general principle. Or perhaps the general principle was valid when you incorporated it, but things have changed. It is important to examine principles before using them to maintain their accuracy.

Deduction Trap 2: Fact vs. Belief as a Premise

Another trap is failing to examine the basis for a premise. A premise based on fact and one based on belief are very different things. A premise based on fact can be judged for accuracy; it can be tested to see if it is faulty. A premise based on belief, however, cannot be tested for accuracy. For example, the continuing debate about abortion can be traced directly to differences in beliefs about when human life begins. Pro-life advocates believe that human life begins at conception; they use this premise to reason that the aborting of a fetus is murder. In contrast, pro-choice advocates believe that a unique human life does not begin until later; they use this premise to reason that terminating a fetus is no more murder than having another part of one's body surgically removed. The arguments on each side of the debate follow logically from their general premises. Neither side is more logical than the other. The differences in their conclusions do not result from faulty logic; instead, the differences result from different major premises. Who is right? It is less a matter of accuracy than of belief, because no objective standard for truth is available on this issue.

Another example of a belief premise is perhaps the most fundamental principle of all of human existence: Is there a supreme being, and if so, what is his or her form? In this case again, no objective standard for truth is available, but this does not mean that we cannot formulate major premises. It does mean that the major premises are based on belief.

Using a general principle that has a foundation in belief as if it rested on a factual foundation is a trap. This is not to say that belief principles are less important than factual principles. To the contrary, belief principles are usually *more* important than factual principles, because belief principles deal with the biggest questions of life: love, happiness, what it means to be human, personal goals in life, and how to treat other people. Don't try to transform your belief principles into factual ones. Recognize your belief principles for what they are. Then examine them to make sure they are what you really believe and not something that you have accepted simply because other people believe them.

Deduction Trap 3: Irrelevant Major Premise

Another trap is working with a major premise that is not a good classification rule for the minor premise. The major premise itself might be clear and might be a good rule in many circumstances, but if it does not express a good classification rule *for your particular purposes,* it will result in a faulty conclusion. For example, let's change the Socrates syllogism a bit to read:

> All men are mortal.
> Socrates is not a man (he's my dog!).

If we use the major premise to classify the mortality of Socrates, we might conclude that Socrates is not mortal through the following reasoning process: Because Socrates is *not* a man, and because all men are mortal, Socrates must *not* be mortal. The wrong general premise leads to a wrong conclusion. We could go back and look for a better major premise, such as *All living things are mortal.* This would be a relevant general premise and therefore support a better process of deduction, where we would conclude that Socrates, the dog, is mortal.

Let's consider another example of this trap—one where the error is not so obvious. Let's say you read the results of a research study that says the most intelligent people of the past several generations have chosen careers in business rather than politics. With this as a major premise, you consider the intelligence of the current U.S. president and conclude that he is not very smart. This conclusion is easy to arrive at, and many people have done so! Now let's look more carefully at the major premise. It claims that the *most* intelligent people do not go into politics, but it does not say that *all* intelligent people avoid politics. Perhaps all people with IQs above 130 go into business rather than politics. The major premise then would say nothing about people with IQs of 130 or below. Let's say the president has an IQ of 125—that would place him in the top one percent of the population. He would not be as smart as the geniuses, but he would be smarter than 99 percent of the population. The point here is to analyze major premises by breaking them down into components and evaluating those elements for accuracy.

Many people do not want to expend the mental effort to think carefully about their major premises. They would rather force a conclusion out of unchecked principles. This holds out the promise of efficiency, but it results in faulty conclusions. Ask yourself: Am I really better off saving time and energy if all I am doing is reaching faulty conclusions?

Irrelevant major premise
When the general principle in a syllogism does not relate to your minor premise.

Deduction Trap 4: Too Simple a Major Premise

Sometimes a major premise is **too simple** to provide a foundation for a deductive reasoning process. This is the case where an event has multiple causes and none of those causes is sufficient. For example, we all probably accept the principle that students need to study to do well on exams. That is the major premise here:

> In order to do well on an exam, Sara must study.
> Sara studied.
> Therefore Sara will do well on the exam.

Too simple a major premise
When the general principle in a syllogism does not contain enough elements to form a complete foundation for reasoning to an accurate conclusion.

Perhaps Sara studied and did *not* do well on the exam. Perhaps Sara studied the wrong material. Perhaps Sara did not study enough. Studying by itself does not guarantee success on an exam; many other factors are involved. Also, studying may not even be a *necessary* condition. Some students can do well on a test without studying for it. These students have one or more other factors that could explain test success, such as a great deal of background knowledge, attending all class lectures and concentrating during class, or taking an easy exam.

It is important to analyze major premises by breaking them down into components. If you find some components missing, then you need to add them to the premise so that it can support a complete deductive process. In the example above, the major premise could be changed to read: *In order to do well on an exam, Sara must study, have good notes to study from, and have good study skills.* From the minor premise of "Sara studied," we cannot conclude how well Sara will do on the exam, because there is no information on the other components of the major premise. The major premise requires more information in the minor premise. Once we observe Sara's preparation more carefully, we can draw a more accurate conclusion about her likely performance on the exam. When a premise contains more than one element, we need to employ conditional reasoning (see the conditional reasoning heuristic below).

HEURISTICS

The traps presented above had to do with the premises used in the deductive reasoning process. The heuristics presented below focus more on the process of reasoning.

Deduction Heuristic 1: Probability Premise

Sometimes a premise is not absolute—it is about some or most of a group, rather than all of the group. An example is *Most people who live in San Francisco are Democrats.* Suppose you meet Sally and find out she lives in San Francisco. If you use the major premise and forget the adjective "most" (thus treating the premise as an absolute), you will conclude that Sally is a Democrat. This conclusion could be a mistake. Sally could be a Republican, an independent, or many other non-Democrat things.

Frequently major premises are not absolute; they allow for exceptions. When a statement uses words such as "many," "most," or "almost all," it allows for exceptions. In essence, it says that the rule holds most of the time but not always. Statements like this are called probabilistic statements. If you follow the rule in your reasoning process, you are likely to be right—the **probability** is on your side. However, you could be wrong.

Probability premise
A major premise that expresses a principle that is likely but not certain to hold.

Probabilistic statements are better than nothing; they help to reduce uncertainty even though they are sometimes wrong. In everyday life many of our conclusions have trivial consequences, so being wrong is not disastrous. In many cases, we have chances to correct our conclusions; for example, if you were talking with Sally after first meeting her, you might draw a wrong conclusion, but you could correct it very quickly.

However, if you are trying to reason toward a conclusion that will have major consequences, you need to reject the goal of efficiency and replace it with the goal of accuracy. In this case, probabilistic statements can pose serious problems, so it is important to try to find an absolute statement to use instead. When it is not possible to find an absolute statement—and this is often the case—then you need to determine the level of probability in your probabilistic statement.

Not all levels of probability are the same. For example, the word "most" could mean 51 percent or 99 percent—that makes a huge difference in the level of confidence you will have in your conclusions. By seeking out percentages, you can make the major premise more precise. Then when you arrive at the conclusion, you should state the confidence you have in your conclusion. In the example of Sally, if you knew that 70 percent of all the registered voters in San Francisco are Democrats and that Sally is registered to vote in San Francisco, you could conclude that there is a 70 percent probability that Sally is a Democrat.

Scientists often report probability values for their conclusions. That is part of their training as scientists. In the physical or social sciences, conclusions usually include p-values (probability values). If you are in the humanities or the arts, you rarely see things quantified like this. However, even outside the sciences there are times when quantities are useful. For example, let's say you have an assignment to do a term paper. It would help if you knew what the probabilities of earning an A would be if you put 10 hours of work into the paper or if you put 50 hours of work into it. If you knew these probabilities accurately, you could plan your time in the most efficient manner to achieve your goals.

Some real-life decisions benefit from precise probabilities. For example, let's say you are considering laser surgery to correct your vision and the doctor tells you that "most" people see much better after the laser surgery, whereas the rest go blind. You would certainly want to know what she meant by "most." Would you have the surgery if she said that "most" meant 54 percent? What if she said that "most" meant 99.999 percent? When your conclusions have major consequences, you need precise and accurate probability figures in your major premise. The probabilities translate into the degree of confidence you can have in your conclusions.

Deduction Heuristic 2: Conditional Reasoning

Not all syllogisms follow a categorical or linear reasoning process. Some follow a **conditional reasoning** process. Conditions are "if" statements. An example of conditional reasoning is:

> If Harry misses any of his math classes, he will not pass his midterm exam.
> Harry passed his midterm exam.
> Therefore, Harry did not miss any of his math classes.

In this syllogism, the first statement is the major premise; it is also the condition. Harry passed his midterm exam because this condition was met. So far so good. But what if Harry had failed his midterm exam? In this case, can we say that he must have missed some of his math classes? The answer is no, because other conditions are necessary for passing, and these other conditions are not included in the major premise. In other words, this condition may not be a *sufficient* condition to pass the midterm—just showing up for class may not be enough to ensure Harry's

Conditional reasoning
Using logic to arrive at an accurate conclusion when the major premise is a conditional one.

success. Perhaps there were three necessary conditions for Harry to pass his midterm: He would need to go to all classes, he would need to have a tutor explain the difficult material to him, and he would need to study on his own for at least 20 hours. Because all three of these conditions are necessary, then Harry must meet all three in order to pass. Meeting only one or two of them is not good enough. Therefore, to avoid this type of trap in reasoning, we must ensure that the major premise includes either (a) a sufficient condition or (b) the full set of necessary conditions.

Conditional reasoning requires special care; often it is only a one-way street and we find ourselves driving the wrong way. For example, consider the following two premises:

If Harry misses any math classes, he will not pass the midterm.
Harry did not miss any math classes.

Can we conclude that Harry passed his midterm? The answer is no, because the premise only says that missing class will lead to failure—it says nothing about attendance necessarily leading to passing the midterm. Here the relationship flows only one way. Missing a math class will guarantee a failure, but attending all math classes will not guarantee a pass. In short, missing a math class is a sufficient condition for failure, but attending all math classes is only a necessary (not a sufficient) condition to pass. To guarantee a pass, Harry must not only go to all classes, but he must also meet some other necessary conditions.

Conditional reasoning can also incorporate probabilistic statements. For example, let's say you are in a psychology course where the professor gives 10 weekly quizzes, each worth 10 points. At the end of the course, the professor sums all the points you earned and assigns you a grade based on the traditional grading scale (90 to 100 is an A; 80 to 89 is a B; 70 to 79 is a C; 60 to 69 is a D; and below 60 points is an E or F). Suppose you earn a 10 on each of the first two quizzes. Can you assess the probability that you will receive an A in the course? You could try, but your guess would not be very good because it is too early in the course and you do not have enough information yet. In contrast, suppose you earn only a 3 on the first quiz and a 6 on the second quiz. You have enough information now to compute that the probability of earning an A is zero, because even if you earn the full 10 on all of the remaining eight quizzes, your total will only sum to 89, and that is not in the A range.

Deduction Heuristic 3: Try to Be Rational

People sometimes do not let themselves use rational reasoning. At times like these, people may be emotional and unable to get around the emotions to see things more clearly—or if they do see things clearly, they still cannot make themselves behave in a rational manner. For example, there are many people who have seen the movie *Jaws*, and the images have scared them so badly that they immediately constructed a general rule: *If I go in the water, I will put myself at high risk for being attacked by a shark.* When these people find themselves in water, they immediately fear a shark attack. This may happen when they are swimming in a lake, and they *know* that sharks are salt-water creatures and are never found in fresh-water lakes. With some people, the general principle is so strong that they apply it even when they are swimming in a backyard pool.

There are many other examples of how the emotion of fear (or the lack of it) leads people to reason irrationally from general principles and thus greatly overestimate (or underestimate) their risk in many situations. One was mentioned earlier: people who fear the risk from dental X-rays yet willingly tolerate the risk from smoking cigarettes. Smokers greatly underestimate the impact of their habit on their health, whereas people who do not like going to the dentist greatly overestimate the impact of X-rays on their health.

Emotions such as love or lust can also affect people's willingness to be rational. We all have dating rules for ourselves, such as: *I will not date someone who* . . . has a history of bad behavior, . . . has hurt you before, . . . was introduced to you by your mother, . . . has served time in prison more than once. Then you meet someone whom your rule tells you not to date—but who attracts you so much that you do it anyway.

Deduction Heuristic 4: Build Knowledge Structures

The best thing you can do to prepare yourself to succeed with the skill of deduction is to build knowledge structures on as many topics as possible. Think of college as the place to acquire many general principles on many different topics. College does this in two ways. One way is by teaching what those general principles are. Professors are experts in their fields, and they pass on key knowledge to students. However, they cannot pass on *all* the general principles you will need in life. There are too many of them. Also, some of the principles change over time. So the second way that education can help you acquire the general principles is by showing you how to construct them for yourself by using induction. Recall from the previous chapter that induction is inferring general principles that identify patterns. Through experience you will notice patterns and make inferences about all sorts of things. These inferences stay with you in your knowledge structures, and you can use them later as major premises in the process of deduction.

In essence, the college experience is a four-year opportunity to expose yourself to many different bodies of knowledge so that you can construct a wide variety of knowledge structures as a strong foundation for any kind of career. However, the irony is that most students regard breadth as something to be avoided, so they instead pursue a much narrower set of courses that will prepare them for an entry-level job in a career they think they would like (even though they often have no direct experience in that type of career). Take these four years to explore a wide range of experiences before locking yourself into a 40-year-plus career path.

EXERCISE 7.1

PRACTICE AT DEDUCTION

1. Which of the following major premises are faulty?
   A. All people from Alabama have southern accents.
   B. All welfare recipients are ethnic minorities.
   C. All days end in darkness.

D. All medical doctors are competent.

E. All college professors have earned a Ph.D.

F. All dogs are mammals.

2. Consider the following syllogism:
Successful students study hard.
Harry works hard.

Can we conclude that Harry is successful? Is the major premise relevant to the minor premise—that is, are working hard and studying hard the same thing?

3. Consider the following syllogisms and decide which are faulty. It might be helpful to draw a Venn diagram to help you "see" the relationships.

Healthy people work out every day.
Harry is healthy.
Harry works out every day.

Some criminals are in jail.
No blondes are criminals.
There are no blondes in jail.

All cats have nine lives.
Cats are mammals.
Mammals have nine lives.

4. Consider the following sets of statements. For each set, decide whether the last statement can be deduced from the other statements, and if so, whether it is accurate.

The chair is to the left of the table.
The lamp is to the right of the table.
The lamp is to the right of the chair.

Molly is a faster runner than Brianna.
Brianna is a slower runner than Daisy.
Molly is a faster runner than Sarah.
Daisy is a faster runner than Molly.

CONCLUSION

The skill of deduction is easy to apply in very simple situations. However, the world often presents fairly complex problems. Deduction can be used to solve even the most complex problems, if we can make the right observations and employ the right general principles.

The key to using deduction well is to cut through the complexity of problems to find their central essence and express it in a major premise and a minor premise. With these in place you can proceed to a deduced conclusion. Accuracy is also important, especially in decisions that will have a significant influence on your life. To achieve greater accuracy, be very careful in identifying a general major premise, and clearly understand the relationship between the major and the minor premises. Finally, to make your reasoning more precise, be clear about whether the reasoning requires a categorical, a conditional, or a linear judgment.

Many scholars treat deductive reasoning as the strongest part of human thought, the epitome of rationality, and the foundation of logic. This type of thought emulates a computer—systematic, logical, and rational. Although the deductive process appears logical and simple on the surface, many hidden traps can render the process faulty or very complex. When the deductive problem is fully specified and people avoid the traps, the solutions will be consistently accurate.

Humans get into trouble with the deductive thinking process when problems are partially specified, so that the application of a computer-like algorithm breaks down. However, unlike computers, humans can muddle through by using heuristics. This is one of the wonderful things about being human. When we don't have enough information to solve a problem, we can go outside the problem to get what we need. In this way we are very different from computers.

The more we learn about how the brain functions, the more we come to realize that the brain is *not* a logical computer. In his book *How the Mind Works,* Steven Pinker (1997) contrasts human brains with computers in this way: "Computers are serial, doing one thing at a time; brains are parallel, doing millions of things at once. Computers are fast; brains are slow. Computer parts are reliable; brain parts are noisy. Computers have a limited number of connections; brains have trillions. Computers are assembled according to a blueprint; brains must assemble themselves." This does not mean that computers are superior to the human brain. In many ways, the human brain is far superior to any computer.

Skill 5: Grouping

LEARNING OBJECTIVES

By reading this chapter, you will:

1. Learn how to develop your skill of grouping.
2. Understand how to use four types of heuristics to help you with the skill of grouping.
   - Emerging classification scheme
   - Number of groups
   - Multiple characteristics
   - Non-categorical schemes
3. Understand how to avoid two traps that can prevent you from using the skill of grouping well.
   - Everything is the same
   - Everything is different

We humans have a lot of experience with grouping things. When we see an unfamiliar object, we use the characteristics of things we have already learned about to make a guess at what the object is—that is, to which category of things it belongs. Often, people who are new to an area will choose a wrong or peripheral characteristic to make the classification, and the classification will be wrong. If someone experienced in classification—such as a parent—is around to correct us, we get better at grouping through a process of trial and error. Over time, we come to understand the essential characteristics of things in different categories.

The key to grouping lies in being aware of classification rules and the characteristics in elements that relate to those rules. Classification rules specify the characteristics an element must have in order for it to be put into a particular group. For example, consider an element that has the following characteristics: it is an animal that is four-legged, is black, has two eyes, has a pointed nose, is as tall as my knee, is wagging its tail, and is wearing a collar with a leash hanging from it. You would likely classify this as a dog. How did you make such a classification? You took into consideration all the details, and those details fit the classification rules for dog (which means there was nothing in the details that did not fit the classification rules for dog). However, some of the details were of more use than others. The first detail—animal—let you rule out many groups, such as inanimate object or plant. "Four-legged" allowed you to rule out all bipeds. Black is a peripheral characteristic not critical in this classification task. "Two eyes" could be relevant, but at this point in the reasoning process it added no useful information. "Pointed nose" rules out cats, as does the height. Finally, the wagging tail and collar with a leash indicate that the animal is domesticated.

The grouping skill works closely with the skills of deduction and induction, which you learned about in the previous two chapters. When the classification rules are clear, then the grouping task requires simple deduction. The rules become the major premise and the characteristics of the elements become the minor premises. The reasoned conclusion is the grouping. In contrast, when the classification rules are *not* clear, then the grouping task requires induction, which means you must look for patterns in the messages in a group, then infer the pattern. In order to infer a pattern, you look at the characteristics shared by the messages in a group, then look at the characteristics shared by messages outside the group to see how they differ. Thus, in order to use the grouping skill well, you have to be skilled at induction and deduction.

Contrasting and comparing are two processes in grouping. *Contrasting* is looking for differences across elements; these differences are what you use to place the elements in different groups. *Comparing* is looking for commonalities across elements; these commonalities are what you use to argue that the elements you have in the same group do in fact belong together.

THE GROUPING ALGORITHM

Grouping is essentially comparing elements to determine how they are alike and contrasting elements to determine how they are different. This skill allows you to reduce a relatively large number of elements down to a smaller set of meaningful groups, which helps you deal with the flow of information more efficiently. You can also use this skill to see which of the characteristics among elements are the most meaningful—you identify the characteristics that make the most difference in linking elements together or setting them apart. When you use this skill well, you significantly enhance your understanding of the nature of the elements.

The following six-step algorithm gives the full process of grouping in a simplified form. If you have a fully specified problem, then you can begin with the fifth step. However, if you have a partially specified problem, you will likely need to begin at the first step in order to develop your own classification scheme, determine the purpose of your grouping, and write your own decision rules.

Step 1: List Classification Schemes

The first step in the process of grouping is to list all possible **classification schemes** that could guide the grouping of message elements. As with the skills of analysis and evaluation, it is best to begin by examining your options before committing to one purpose.

Classification scheme
A grouping of elements based on their similarities and differences.

For example, look at Figure 8.1. These objects can be grouped in several different ways. One way is by color, resulting in three groups: red, blue, and green. Or we could group them by shape, in three groups: triangle, circle, and square. Or we could group by size, in one group of larger objects and a second group of smaller objects. Thus there are three obvious classification schemes: color, shape, and size. Perhaps you can think of another classification scheme to group the objects in Figure 8.1.

As another example, let's consider the classification schemes that we could use to compare and contrast messages from the media—specifically, the magazines *Newsweek, Cosmopolitan,* and *Soldier of Fortune.* If we were to compare

The Skill of Grouping

Purpose: To determine which elements are alike in some way and which elements are different in some way.
Pre-Task: Conduct an analysis to identify message elements.
Process:
1. List all possible classification schemes that could guide the grouping of message elements.
2. Determine your purpose for comparing/contrasting.
3. Select the most appropriate classification scheme(s) to fulfill your purpose.
4. Formulate the decision rule.
5. Use the classification scheme to place each message element in its proper category. At this point you have conducted a one-level analysis.
6. Examine the configuration in the groupings.

Figure 8.1   Classifying objects.

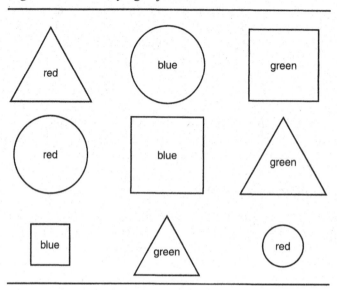

and contrast the stories in these three magazines, we would find differences in editorial perspective, business constraints, and audience. We could also classify stories by time (to see if the stories change somehow issue to issue), region (does the story appear the same way in all regional issues of the magazine?), or location (do certain kinds of stories appear in the front or in the back of each issue?). There are many, many possibilities for classification schemes. If you have difficulty identifying a classification scheme, try the emerging classification scheme heuristic discussed later in this chapter.

Step 2: Determine Your Purpose

Once you understand the options for your grouping, the second step is to choose a purpose to guide your comparing and contrasting. As with the task of analysis and evaluation, grouping is a tool that needs a plan or goal to guide it. Ask yourself why you are doing the grouping. Typically the grouping task is guided by the dimensions you used to analyze the information (see the section on analysis in Chapter 4).

Step 3: Select the Classification Scheme

The third step is to select the most appropriate classification scheme(s) to fulfill your purpose. There are almost always many classification schemes to consider, but not all of them are equally useful. As you consider which one to select, keep in mind the purpose for the grouping.

Let's consider an example. Imagine that I show you three objects: a red ball, a pear, and a knife. Then I ask you which of the three objects is most closely associated with an apple. You could pick the red ball, saying that they share the same shape and color. Or you could pick the pear, reasoning that both are examples of fruit. Or you could pick the knife, because you use a knife to pare the apple before eating it; thus the knife is associated with the apple by function. Which of these three is correct? They all are, because there is a reason to associate each one with the apple. At this point the problem of selection is partially specified, because many correct answers are possible, and there is no way to determine which is the best one.

To make this problem more fully specified, think of a context in which you might be asked this question. Let's say I asked this question in a nutrition class. The answer would be the pear, because they are both fruit and, therefore, the apple's nutrients most closely match that of the pear. However, if I asked this question in a drawing class, the answer would be the red ball, because the apple's shape and color most closely match the ball.

Here's another example. Suppose you examine 20 newspaper ads for political candidates. One classification scheme could be by the political party of the candidate. This would be a good classification scheme if you were doing this as a project for a political science class. Another classification scheme could be by type of appeal (issues, personality, patriotism, record, etc.); this would be a useful classification scheme for an advertising class. Another classification scheme could be by type of layout (pictures, graphics, text, etc.); this would be a useful classification scheme for a graphic design class. There are many other elements that you could use for a classification scheme. Notice that the usefulness of a scheme depends on the context and purpose of the classification task. While a classification scheme based on political party is a useful scheme in a political science class, it is not likely to be helpful in a graphic design class.

Step 4: Formulate Your Decision Rule

In this step, you list the categories in your classification scheme and write a set of rules that would guide people to place messages in the right category. These rules need to be very clear so that a person would place each message in one and only one group and do so with confidence.

Now, suppose for classifying the political ads you decide to go with the scheme of party affiliation. To do the fourth step, you would go back through the ads to see how many categories you need. You notice that in each of the ads, the candidate is either a Democrat or a Republican; there are no independents or candidates from other parties. Your **decision rule** would be: *When a message (the ad) features a Democratic candidate, it goes into the Democrat group; if the message features a Republican candidate, it goes into the Republican group.* Notice that your decision rule is clear enough so that you can put every message into one and only one group. This example is a rather simple one. Let's try another example that is a bit more involved.

Decision rule
A rule for how to categorize messages based on their characteristics.

Let's say you want to group the 20 newspaper ads for political candidates by how they are laid out, so you focus on the components of their design. You notice that all of the 20 ads have text, but that some also have pictures and some also have graphics. So you devise the following categories: (1) text only, (2) text plus pictures, (3) text plus graphics, and (4) text plus pictures and graphics. These four categories encompass all possible combinations of text, pictures, and graphics that you found in the 20 ads. Next you must write a set of decision rules to guide the placement of ads into their proper categories. This is more challenging than it might first appear. For example, what is the difference between a picture and a graphic? A photograph is clearly a picture, but what if an artist has drawn a picture of the candidate—is that a picture or a graphic? What if a computer artist has morphed the candidate's head into a pie chart and labeled each slice of the pie as how the candidate has voted to spend public money—is that a graphic or a picture? Designers of ads can be very creative, so the differences between pictures, graphics, text, and other elements can blur. This makes writing clear classification rules more challenging.

The task in this example can be made even more challenging. Let's say you want to categorize the ads in terms of how big the picture image is. You could use categories for big, medium, and small, but then you would have to decide how big a picture has to be for each category (see the non-categorical scheme heuristic later in this chapter). Or what if you want to categorize ads on some dimension of aesthetic quality? This would require an evaluative judgment about each ad's aesthetics. Categorization schemes that require evaluative judgments are even more challenging to design. However, the steps in the algorithm are still useful. The difference between a simple scheme and a more complex scheme essentially comes down to the degree of challenge in constructing categories and writing clear rules to guide the classifications.

Step 5: Categorize Elements

If you have been careful in the first four steps, this step should be fairly automatic. You look for the key characteristic in a message as specified by each decision rule. If you find that characteristic in the message, you follow the rule and include that message in the group; if you do not find that characteristic in the message, you exclude the message from the group. Perform this categorization process for each message. Those messages that are in the same group have been compared; they all share the same key characteristic(s). The messages that differ by grouping have been contrasted; they differ on the key characteristic(s).

Step 6: Examine Groupings

The final step in applying the grouping skill is to check your groupings to see if they make sense. Sometimes we get so wrapped up in the details of placing individual messages into groups that we lose sight of the big picture. Once your groupings are done, stand back and see if there are any messages in a group that do not look like they belong there. For example, if you are grouping television shows on the characteristic of degree of violence, you will have one category labeled "highly violent" that includes crime programs and action/adventure shows. But this same category is likely to include some cartoons, *The Jerry Springer Show,* and some local news programs. You must ask yourself if this grouping makes sense. If the answer is yes, then you need to be clear about your reasoning so that you can defend your groupings to possible critics. If the answer is no—the messages in that one group do not all belong together—then you need to re-examine your decision rules. Were you sloppy in using a decision rule to place messages into groups? Or was the decision rule itself faulty?

HEURISTICS

The skill of grouping appears very simple. After all, people seem to be able to use this skill at a very early age. Even toddlers group people (strangers and familiar people), things (those that move and those that do not), and places (home and not-home).

As people grow older, they are constantly faced with grouping tasks. Many of these tasks are fairly challenging, although they may not appear so until we really examine them. For example, few people have a problem classifying objects as being either a chair or not a chair. Yet we never learned a formal definition for chair, nor did we learn any formal process that would guide the classification. This claim may sound faulty, but try writing down your definition for chair. Then use what you have on the paper to classify things like stools, ottomans, rocking chairs, high chairs, armchairs, wing-back chairs, folding chairs, three-legged chairs, beanbag chairs, benches, chaise lounges, couches, loveseats, and recliners. You will notice that although you fully understand the concept of chair and can make endless decisions without error in classifying objects as a chair or not, it is still extremely difficult to articulate a good definition. Classifying objects as being a chair or not is a partially specified problem. We have no decision-making flow chart that can guide such a classification task.

We use many heuristics with the skill of grouping. In fact, without heuristics, we would not be able to complete many grouping tasks at all. The importance of heuristics became apparent when scientists working on artificial intelligence (AI) began programming computers to emulate the human mind and found the task of grouping to be an enormously challenging one. Computers are programmed with algorithms and slavishly follow those programmed rules. However, when a computer does not have enough rules to complete a task, it gets stuck and cannot finish the task. The computer cannot figure out a way out of a dead-end. It cannot think laterally or acquire information through intuition or insight. Humans can do these things and thus can complete very challenging grouping tasks. But in order to do this, we need heuristics. This section presents four heuristics that can help with the most common challenges of using the grouping skill.

Grouping Heuristic 1: Emerging Classification Scheme

There may be times when you can think of no classification schemes for a grouping task. A classification scheme is essential—you cannot develop a list of categories and classification rules without one. So you must develop the scheme while you are doing the grouping. This—the **emerging classification scheme**—is the most challenging form of the grouping task.

To illustrate this, let's say you attend the first meeting of each of 10 courses at your university, and you want to group the professors in those courses in terms of the messages they present about themselves. To start to develop a category scheme, you take notes on what each of the 10 professors say about themselves. You read your notes and look for differences and similarities in their messages. Let's say you notice that a few of the professors say nothing at all about themselves. Of those who

Emerging classification scheme

A classification scheme that you develop as you examine elements in messages and not in advance.

do reveal things about themselves, you notice that some limit their remarks to their role as a professor; they talk about what they hope to achieve in the course and tell stories about how they designed the course and what kinds of student behavior make them happy. The other professors seem to get more personal and tell stories about their family and their interests outside of teaching. Thus, three categories emerge from your notes: nothing personal, personal teaching, and personal life. Now you need to ask yourself what your purpose for the classification is. If these three categories are enough for your purpose, you end up with a three-category scheme. However, if these three categories do not get at what you are trying to achieve, then you need to look for other categories. You need to re-analyze your notes and look for something else. Perhaps you could group on the substance of what they said. Some professors may have talked for an hour without saying much, while others may have had so many valuable things to say that your hand cramped up while you took notes.

The challenge with this heuristic is building the scheme while you are doing the comparing and contrasting. The classification scheme becomes a product of the grouping process itself. Thus the process of grouping is cyclical. The more you examine the elements in the messages, the more you understand your options for categories, and as you work with the options, you become more clear about the best option and about your purpose. With a clearer purpose, you are better able to construct categories and decision rules.

Grouping Heuristic 2: Number of Groups

How many groups should you end up with? It is impossible to answer this question in a general way. It depends on the elements you are trying to group. If those elements only have one characteristic and that characteristic has only two possible values, then you really only have two possibilities for grouping. For example, let's say you have a dozen batteries lying on your desk. You would want to group these objects according to whether they have any power left or not. If they work, you put them in one pile and save them. If they do not work, you put them in another pile and throw them away.

Besides whether they work or not, the batteries also have a size (AAAA, AAA, AA, A, B, C, D, etc.), a brand (such as Eveready, Duracell, Energizer), and a voltage rating (such as 1.5 volts, 9 volts). Once you have selected a characteristic on which to group, the values available on that characteristic will limit the number of groups you could have.

While the number of values on a particular characteristic will usually determine the number of groups, some elements may have no obvious number of values. In this situation, the number of groups is likely to be determined by your purpose for the classification. This brings us to the next heuristic.

Grouping Heuristic 3: Multiple Characteristics

The simplest form of comparing/contrasting is to make decisions on only one key characteristic. When you do your grouping on one characteristic, your comparing and contrasting process is likely to result in a fairly simple and easily defended set of elements.

Sometimes it makes more sense to consider more than one characteristic simultaneously. However, the grouping task becomes more complex with each additional characteristic. With only one characteristic guiding the grouping, it is easy to envision the groups; you can draw a line and plot the elements in one dimension. With two characteristics guiding the grouping, it is a bit more complicated but still relatively simple: draw a graph with one characteristic on the horizontal axis and the other on the vertical axis. With more than two characteristics, it becomes very difficult to envision or list the groupings.

Let's consider an example. Suppose you want to compare/contrast American universities. You could group according to whether each university is public or private. That would be one characteristic. You could also group by tuition (high, medium, or low). That would be a second characteristic. You could also group by rejection rate (high, medium, or low). That would be a third characteristic.

However, let's say that you want to group the universities as "best buys" to determine where you would get the best value for your money. To do this, you would need to group on the two characteristics of cost and benefits (see Figure 8.2).

Notice that it is important to group not on cost alone and not on benefits alone, but on costs and benefits simultaneously. If you grouped only on cost, you would come up with a group of relatively expensive universities (A, B, and C) that all would be very similar in cost, but would differ dramatically in benefits. Also, universities G and H are similar in cost, but H provides many more benefits than G. If you grouped only on benefits, you would put universities C and H together. Although they belong together on benefits, they are radically different in cost. As this example illustrates, grouping on a single dimension can be misleading. When the elements to be grouped have several important characteristics, it is usually better to group on all of them, especially when the grouping decision is an important one.

To make a more refined grouping of the universities, consider that the element of benefits would itself be composed of several sub-elements (e.g., faculty–student ratio, number of majors and courses offered, percentage of students going to graduate school or professional careers of their choice). A grouping based on all of these characteristics would provide lots of information for your decision.

There are two major challenges in using a classification scheme with **multiple characteristics.** One challenge is to determine which characteristics should be included in the classification scheme. Obviously, there are many ways to define a benefit of college. Would you include only academic benefits, such as the classes, professors, library, and computers? Would you include non-academic benefits, such as quality of the dorms, number and kind of social clubs, sports activities, and the weather? Would you limit yourself to the benefits that matter only while you are actually in school, or would you include outcomes such as ability to get a job and earning level five years after graduation? In addition, the cost characteristic also suggests sub-elements: tuition, room and board, and miscellaneous charges (fees not included in tuition).

The second challenge of using a classification scheme with multiple characteristics is to make a summary judgment. Should all the characteristics have equal weight? As you evaluate universities, perhaps the cost factors should be weighted

Multiple characteristics
Guideline for considering more than one thing about each message when trying to put it into a category.

Figure 8.2   Example of simultaneous grouping: costs and benefits.

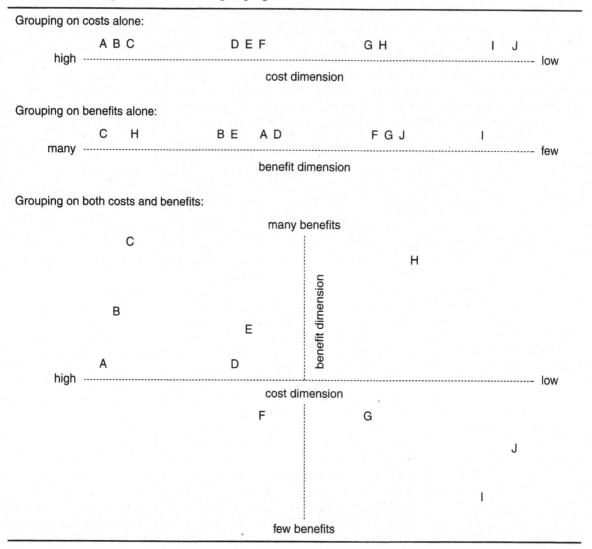

about the same as the benefit factors, but within the cost factors, perhaps tuition should be weighted most heavily. Maybe the presence of one characteristic cancels out the effect of another characteristic. A university might have many academic and non-academic benefits on campus, but the graduates may find it difficult to get jobs or get into graduate schools. The students' lack of success after graduation might cancel out the benefits on campus.

Adding more elements to the cost–benefit equation makes the development of classification rules more difficult, especially if each of the elements has a different weight. This extra effort is often worthwhile, however, because it allows you to make good decisions that are grounded in good reasoning.

Grouping Heuristic 4: Non-Categorical Schemes

Sometimes the characteristic upon which you build your classification scheme is **not categorical**—that is, it comes in different amounts or levels rather than distinctly different types or quantities. In this case you have three options: (1) group all elements that have any level of the characteristic together, (2) group elements with less than the full amount of the characteristic along with elements that have none of the characteristic, or (3) create a middle category for elements that have some but not all of the characteristic. If you choose option #3, then you have the challenge of deciding if all elements that have some of the characteristic belong in the same group; some of those elements may have a lot while other elements may have only a little of the characteristic. Should you have several middle categories? If so, how many middle categories? The challenge here is to transform a continuum of degrees of the characteristic into a set of categories.

> **Non-categorical scheme**
> A guideline for grouping when the classification scheme does not have natural categories.

To illustrate this type of challenge, let's say you want to group front-page newspaper stories on the characteristic of length. There is no natural category system for short, medium, and long length. Instead, there is a natural continuum. You could create categories by arbitrarily cutting up the continuum—for example, short articles are one to five column inches, medium stories are over five but less than 12 column inches, and long stories are 12 column inches or longer. Thus you have overcome the lack of a natural category system by creating your own set of categories.

However, this category scheme might bother you because it is arbitrary—that is, why should a story that is five column inches be considered short, while a story of six column inches is considered medium? There is no way to eliminate the arbitrary nature of translating a natural continuum into categories. However, you can make it seem less arbitrary by constructing the categories in a way that relates to natural groupings in the elements.

To find natural groupings in the newspaper stories, you could measure the length of each story and plot these lengths first, before constructing your categories. Let's say you do this and find that there is a cluster of stories at 5 to 7 inches, another cluster at 10 to 12 inches, and a third cluster at 20 to 24 inches. You conclude that there are three groups. Notice that if you had used the first clustering scheme given, you would have divided the cluster at 5 to 7 inches into short and medium-length stories—thus, stories with only minor differences in length would not all be grouped together. At the other end of the continuum, stories of 12 inches and 24 inches (a large difference in length) would both have been classified in the same category (long stories). When you must translate a continuous distribution of characteristics into a categorical classification scheme, it is better to look at how the elements cluster on the continuum before deciding on how many categories you will have and where the boundaries of the categories should be.

AVOIDING TRAPS

The two traps discussed in this section are opposites: sometimes everything looks the same to you and you cannot see more than one group; other times, you cannot see any similarity at all, and each message seems to be its own group.

Both of these are traps if they prevent you from reaching your goal for grouping. No matter how alike all messages at first seem, there are bound to be differences. On the other hand, no matter how unique each message seems, there are always similarities.

To illustrate, let's consider what marketers do in grouping the U.S. population of 280 million people. At the individual level, each of us is unique; no two of us dresses, acts, or thinks identically to anyone else—even twins! In addition to our differences, we share some commonalities. If you were to group people by age, it would make sense to put all people from 15 to 18 years old in one group. You would find lots of commonalities in the way they dress, the music they listen to, and the way they spend their time. Of course, everyone in this age group is not identical, but the commonalities are far more consistent than they would be if you tried to put people 50 to 55 into this same group.

Given any set of elements, it is possible to argue that they are all alike in some way, and it is also possible to argue that they are all different in some way. This is possible as an academic exercise, something that can be interesting to talk about, but when you are faced with a real-life problem, the key is to be aware of your purpose. This will almost always require you to find a reasonable number of groups.

Grouping Trap 1: Everything Seems the Same

At times you will not be able to find ways that messages are different from one another; everything will look the same to you. In this case, try listing all the characteristics that make them look the same. As you make this list, other characteristics may occur to you, and these may show how the messages differ. Let's say this does not happen. What do you do? You can try listing the *opposites* of the characteristics on your list. Now you have two lists. Do any of the messages have characteristics on the "opposite" list? If not, you might need to gather more messages.

If these techniques do not work for you, then try the "elephant technique." Think about an elephant and how it is different from all the elements you are trying to group. For example, suppose you are trying to divide the music of Britney Spears into groups, and all of her songs sound the same to you—that is, you just can't see any differences that would allow you to put her songs into separate groups. So think of something that's *really* different—an elephant. How does an elephant differ from Britney Spears' songs? One way is that an elephant is alive and music is not a living thing. How can this help you group Britney Spears' songs? Perhaps some are livelier than others. You could also think of an elephant moving around; it is slow and ponderous. Perhaps some of Britney Spears' music is slow-paced and other songs are faster. The ground vibrates when an elephant walks. Perhaps some songs have a stronger bass beat than others. The value of the elephant technique is that it gets you far away from the things you are trying to group and gives you a very different perspective on them. The ridiculous comparisons it forces you to make will get you thinking in a lateral way and help you get around the barrier that has trapped your thinking.

You don't have to think about an elephant to use the technique. The "elephant" can be anything that's radically different from the elements you are trying to group. It can be your grandmother's false teeth, the buzzing of a bee, the smell of a month-old slice of pizza, the method of long division, or a French kiss. Be creative with your elephant!

Grouping Trap 2: Everything Seems Different

Some people are overly analytical. Recall from the chapter on knowledge styles that people vary in terms of their conceptual differentiation. Some people tend to group all things together unless those things are very different from one another. Other people like to create lots of neat little groupings. The way a person goes about grouping reveals a lot about his or her personality. Think of your sock drawer. Do you have all your socks thrown in together? Or do you have them lined up according to color, pattern, style, and purpose (dress, casual, athletic)? People with a high need to group and organize keep analyzing the characteristics of things until they find enough to make each item seem unique. On those rare occasions when you want to have the same number of categories as messages, with one and only one message in each category, this tendency could be a good thing. But typically, the reason we group is to end up with a smaller number of groups than messages. This allows us to organize a large number of things (messages) into a small number of categories, for efficiency.

To avoid this trap of seeing every element as unique, focus more on similarities than differences. Randomly choose two elements from all the elements you must group. Force yourself to see something the two elements have in common. Then look to see how many other elements have that same thing in common. If you find that a good percentage of elements have that thing in common, then you could use that characteristic as a classification rule. What is a "good percentage"? Somewhere between 10 percent and 50 percent. If you find more than half the elements share the characteristic, then that characteristic is not a useful basis for grouping. If less than 10 percent share the characteristic, then perhaps it is too trivial a commonality to use as a grouping rule.

EXERCISE 8.1

PRACTICE AT GROUPING

1. Observe how other people group things.

   Go to your professor's office and look at how books are arranged. Are there sections for different kinds of books, or are the books simply in one group arranged alphabetically?

   Look at your roommate's side of the room. There is likely to be a group of things on a desk, another group on a dresser, and another group on a night table. Can you see what all the objects in one group have in common? Can you see why there are differences across groups (why an object obviously belongs in one particular group and not the others)?

   Go to a store that sells magazines. How many groupings of magazines can you identify? Which grouping has the largest number of magazines?

Go to a grocery store and walk down the soft drink aisle. How are the products grouped? By brand? By size? By type (all the diet drinks together, all colas together, etc.)? Why do you think the sodas are grouped the way they are?

2. On a piece of paper, list about a dozen names of friends.

   Arrange those friends in groups. First, group them by gender. This arrangement has two groups. How many other groupings can you think of?

3. On a piece of paper, list all the things you like about college. Arrange those things in groups. How many different arrangements can you make?

4. Think about the student body at your college. Most colleges are mixes of different types of students. For example, one type found at most campuses is athletes.

   How many groups of students can you think of in the student body at your school? For each group, what are the things all students in that group share? List the adjectives that would apply to all members of that group.

   In which student group are you? Do you share most of the characteristics of that group? If so, you are a prototypical member. If you only share a few characteristics with the other members of your group, perhaps you should create a new group with you as its prototypical member. How many members (besides yourself) are there in this new group?

5. Think about how knowledge is organized at your college.

   Think of the physical sciences. How many are there? What are the differences between each of those groups? For example, what makes biology different from chemistry?

   Consider the humanities. How many groups are there within the humanities? What are the differences between those groups?

   Now think of the arts. How many groups are there within the arts? What are the differences between those groups?

   Now think about the bigger picture. You have broken the physical sciences down into groups. You have done the same to the humanities and the arts. If physical sciences, humanities, and the arts are three important groups of knowledge on campus, what are the other important groups?

6. Think about your groupings of students (from #4 above) and your groupings of knowledge (from #5 above).

   Do you see any match between a particular group of students and a particular group of knowledge? If so, what are the characteristics in that student group that match the characteristics of the knowledge group?

7. Think about how you spend your time during a typical day. How many groups would you need to categorize your time? List them.

   For each group, list the activities that count. For example, if "going to class" is one of your groups, does the time spent walking to class count?

Does talking to your professor after class count? Where do you draw the line about what gets put into this group?

For each group, estimate the amount of time you spend on activities in that time group on a typical day.

Test your groups. Tomorrow as you go through your day, write down each thing you do and how much time you spend with it. At the end of the day, arrange those activities and times into your time groups. As you do this, you may decide to modify your rules for what goes into a group; you may even want to rename groups or reconfigure the groups themselves.

CONCLUSION

Grouping is a skill that people use every day. The ways they classify and categorize things are the result of trial and error. A more efficient and successful method is to follow the six-step algorithm presented in this chapter. Because many grouping tasks are partially specified, it is important to take advantage of the heuristics given. A few simple techniques can overcome the typical traps that interfere with grouping.

In formal education, students are likely to learn classification as a set of rules rather than a flexible method. Teachers simply don't have the time to follow students around and give them personal feedback on the process, so they teach rules instead. Some topics—such as math and science—lend themselves to rules, but others, such as the arts, do not. This chapter presented a method that, with practice, you can be successful in applying to any subject.

Skill 6: Synthesis

LEARNING OBJECTIVES

By reading this chapter, you will:

1. Learn how to develop your skill of synthesis.
2. Understand how to use four heuristics to help you with the skill of synthesis.

   ▪ Work with fixed constraints first

   ▪ Too many elements

   ▪ Too few elements

   ▪ Balance systematic and creative thinking

3. Understand how to avoid two traps that can prevent you from using the skill of synthesis well.

   ▪ Too complex

   ▪ Expectation of convergence

Synthesis is the assembling of elements into a complex whole. It is not reassembling of something you took apart; it is not simply putting something back together. If you break a vase and glue all the parts back together, that is not synthesis. Synthesis is assembling pieces so that something new is created. That new thing is a **complex whole.** For example, if you take apart 10 cars, throw away all the bad parts and use the good parts to build a truck out of them, that is synthesis; the complex whole is the truck. The "whole" is the truck, and we refer to it as complex because it is a newly configured vehicle; it is not the same as any of the cars you started with. When we use synthesis with information, the complex whole can be many things, such as a brand-new knowledge structure, an old knowledge structure reconfigured with fresh information into a new and improved knowledge structure, an elaborated opinion, or a fresh solution to an old problem.

Complex whole
A more elaborated whole or reconfigured whole.

A synthesis begins with the skills of analysis and evaluation. Analysis is used to break messages down into their elements. Evaluation is used to judge the value of the elements. Those elements that are judged to have value are the raw materials to use in the assembly of a new message.

Synthesis is the skill we frequently use to incorporate new information into existing knowledge structures. We analyze new messages to identify the key bits of information. Then we evaluate those bits of information for accuracy and to determine if they would be useful to add to an existing knowledge structure. We blend the valued elements with the relevant elements in the existing knowledge structure to construct a newly configured knowledge structure. This is the process we follow when we create a new knowledge structure; we use information from messages as well as other existing knowledge structures to build something new.

As with the other strategic thinking skills, synthesis can be very simple or very complex. A simple example of a synthesis is when a television program breaks for a commercial and we use the break to speculate on what will happen next in the show. We quickly analyze the characters and evaluate their importance to the unfolding action; we ignore the secondary characters and focus instead on the primary characters; we take the pattern of their actions up to this point in the show and project that pattern into the future to guess what they might do next. This is a synthesis because we have used the information we have (the plot up to this point) to build something new (a guess about the rest of the plot we have yet to see). This synthesis is fairly simple and informal; it might take only a few seconds.

A much more challenging form of synthesis would be writing a teleplay for a brand-new series. In order to do this well, you would need to analyze many different television programs to see what elements are available to use for your show. You would need to see what types of characters are most prevalent in successful shows. You would need to analyze how plots get under way, how action develops, the pacing of the action, how plots are resolved, and how dialog is used. You would evaluate all those elements in determining which characters, plots, settings, and themes to use. Then you would need to assemble all these elements into a program. The final product depends on how you assemble all these elements in a new, creative manner.

For another example, let's say you slightly favor a particular politician, but you are not sure if you can strongly support her. You analyze her positions on a wide range of issues, then evaluate her positions on those issues using the criterion of what you believe to be the correct positions. This analysis and evaluation results in two lists: her good positions (those you agree with strongly) and her bad positions (those you disagree with strongly).

What you have done here, in essence, is synthesized a model of your political beliefs. You have a clear list of things you feel strongly positive about and another list of things you feel strongly negative about. You began this effort trying to work through a question about whether this candidate was worthy of your support, and your goal was to decide whether or not to vote for her. However, you ended up with something more valuable: a model of your political beliefs. You clarified your feelings and now have a model you can use as a guide in the search for candidates you can support. Without a clear model of your political beliefs, you are forced into a reactive position. But with a clear model, you are able to be active in seeking what you want.

What models have you synthesized? Do you have a model for a perfect college course? A good professor? A good friend? A perfect date? A loving relationship? An exciting career? If you do not have clear models for these important things, perhaps you are walking around with a constant nagging feeling that the things that are happening to you just don't feel right. Conducting a formal synthesis in these areas will help you clarify your feelings and allow you to act to fulfill your expectations.

THE SYNTHESIS ALGORITHM

The skill of synthesis is always used with partially specified problems. This is because the end point is never clearly known before we begin a synthesis task. Even so, there are some standard steps in the process, an algorithm composed of three steps. However, before the synthesis proper can begin, we need to generate the raw materials for the synthesis by analyzing messages (breaking them down into their component elements) and evaluating those elements.

Step 1: Determine Purpose

The first step is to determine your purpose for the synthesis. Usually the purpose is to solve some sort of problem that bothers you. Here are a few reasons for conducting a synthesis:

- Maybe you have a problem that is a *dilemma:* all the possible solutions are equally bad. You wish you could take the best parts of all those possible solutions and combine them into one option that would have many advantages and none of the disadvantages.
- Perhaps you strongly favor one side of a controversy but you have been exposed to some convincing evidence supporting the other side of the controversy. You don't want to abandon your opinion, and yet you cannot ignore the new evidence.
- Perhaps you are in a relationship that is no longer working for you, but you are not sure what to change in the relationship or in your role that would work better for you.

The Skill of Synthesis

Purpose: To assemble elements into a new structure
Pre-Task: Conduct an evaluation of message elements.
Process:

1. Determine your purpose for the synthesis.
2. Select the message elements with the highest evaluation and discard those that are unacceptable for your purpose.
3. Assemble the selected elements into a whole.
    A. If the whole is complete (attains your goal), you have finished the synthesis.
    B. If the whole is not complete, select elements from the acceptable category of your evaluation and/or create new elements that will fill the gaps and complete the whole.

- You might be confronting a problem that appears too large, too amorphous, too complex, or too dynamic for you to get a handle on it. A synthesis allows you to break the problem down into component parts, evaluate the components in terms of which are bothering you the most, then arrange those components to see the problem more clearly.

Notice that a synthesis is not motivated by a clear goal, such as to develop a solution or opinion. Instead, it is motivated more by a troublesome situation. You undertake the synthesis without knowing how it will turn out, but you have faith that doing the synthesis will make matters better by clarifying things and even taking you all the way to a creative solution that you just cannot imagine when you begin.

Step 2: Select the Best Elements

The second step in synthesis is to select the message elements with the highest evaluation and discard those that are unacceptable. Your criterion for selecting elements is usefulness. Elements that cannot help you achieve your purpose for the synthesis are rejected.

Up to this point, the left brain dominates the task. The more complete and systematic you are with the analysis and evaluation, the better will be your raw materials. Without this preparation, you would have to gather raw materials "on the fly," thinking up the pieces as you need them. The resulting synthesis may look very creative and innovative, but it will usually not be useful because it is not complete, organized, and grounded in the reality of the situation.

If you are not careful and systematic in selecting elements, you will end up with a hodgepodge of all sorts of things. When you try to assemble them into something meaningful, you will probably find that you do not have enough of what you need.

Step 3: Assemble Elements

The third step in the synthesis is to assemble the selected elements into a whole. Think of this as solving a puzzle—but not a picture puzzle, where there is only one picture and therefore only one right way to assemble the elements. Instead, think of this as a building-block puzzle, where there are many ways to put the blocks together. You could use the blocks to build a house, a castle, a tower, a city, or any number of things. The key is to have some vision for what you are building.

With ideas instead of blocks, the task is more abstract, but the principle still applies: Envision your goal. Follow your vision as a guide, but be flexible. Do not treat your vision as a recipe that must be followed no matter what. Remember that your construction is an act of creation, and play with different configurations. Try new things to see how they look.

Frequently ask "What if?" questions and see what happens when you try alternatives. If you try a construction that does not seem to work, then reject it. Learning what does not seem to work is as important to solving your problem as learning what does work. Learn from your mistakes. Only through trial and error can you stumble on to a solution that you could not see before you got started.

Remember that your assembly task is to arrange individual elements so that they work together. If you have elements that do not seem to go together, ask yourself if any of them can be adapted so that they will work together. To use a very concrete example, perhaps you have a plug that won't fit into your wall outlet. Can you get an adapter that will let you use the existing plug and wall outlet? Perhaps some of your elements are like oil and others are like water—they just won't mix together. Can you find a chemical catalyst that you could add to the two and make them congeal? The lesson from these examples is that sometimes you must bring something new to your set of elements to help them work together.

Think structurally. If you have two sets of elements that do not work well together, perhaps you can keep them separate as they move forward on parallel paths until each produces its own product; perhaps those products will be compatible. Or perhaps the elements should occur in a particular sequence, so that everything will fit together in succession. For example, if I served you a dinner that consisted of a plate with a bed of lettuce, soaked in tomato soup, with a scoop of vanilla ice cream floating on it, you would not find this very appetizing, and you would probably think that those three things do not belong together. Of course, they do not belong together on one plate, but they *could* belong together in a dinner of separate courses. If you separate the elements and eat the soup, then the salad, then the ice cream, you might find the combination a delicious meal. Sequence and separation matter.

HEURISTICS

Synthesis Heuristic 1: Work with Fixed Constraints First

The third step of the algorithm does not provide much detail, so you may be confused about how to assemble the elements. The task may seem to be amorphous, and you may be asking: How can I get started? The best way to get started is to

Fixed constraints

Parameters of the problem that are given to you and cannot be changed.

begin with the **fixed constraints.** The fixed constraints are things that cannot be changed. They are the "givens."

For example, if you are trying to decide how to spend your money for Christmas presents, the amount of money you have to spend is likely to be a fixed constraint. If you have ten thousand dollars to spend, you have many more options to consider than if you have only one hundred dollars. If you have only one hundred dollars, do not spend your time thinking about combinations of expensive items, because these options are outside the fixed constraint. Another constraint in this problem is the number of people you must buy for. If you must buy presents for four people, then you know each gift should be about 25 dollars; this narrows down your options and brings more clarity to the process. Another constraint might be that one person is much more important than the other three, so perhaps that special person's gift should cost about fifty dollars and the other fifty dollars should be divided among the remaining three people.

Working with the constraints first gives more structure to your task. You still need to decide what to buy for each person, but at least you know how much you can spend on each, and that simplifies the problem. However, before you accept something as a fixed constraint, challenge it. Perhaps something that appears to be fixed really is not; maybe it can be altered.

Synthesis Heuristic 2: Too Many Elements

The synthesis is completed when it attains your goal. That goal is usually utility—a useful solution to a problem. At times, you will achieve that goal and still have elements of value left over. In that case, you can ask whether the solution's utility would be increased if you added those elements. If so, you may want to modify your synthesis. If not, then ignore those elements, even though you decided they had good value in the evaluation phase of your preparation.

The strongest elements are the ones that receive the highest evaluations. You don't want to ignore these, so begin with them, and give them a central place in the synthesis. If you don't begin with the strongest elements, you may end up constructing something that does not include one or more of these strong elements. This usually means that the elements that are in the synthesis are weaker than what you have left over, resulting in a less useful synthesis.

Synthesis Heuristic 3: Too Few Elements

You might run out of elements before you feel the synthesis is complete. Perhaps you have been able to incorporate all the elements of value from your evaluation process, and yet your synthesis is still missing something—it has gaps in a process or reasoning, or it lacks coherence and doesn't quite make sense. In this case, you need to find new messages and cycle through the planning process again so that you have more elements of value to add to your synthesis. Be careful when you are "adding" these new elements that they are not simply patched in. Instead, they need to be integrated; they need to fit well together to create a coherent whole. For the synthesis to be as useful as possible, each element should contribute to some overall purpose.

Synthesis Heuristic 4: Balance Systematic and Creative Thinking

To perform a synthesis well, you need to use both sides of your brain. The left side provides systematic reasoning, and the right side provides creativity. They should be in balance. If you use the left side of your brain too much, the resulting synthesis will look too much like your old opinion or knowledge structure; there will not be enough new elements to transform it into something fresh. If you use the right side of your brain too much, the resulting synthesis will be too fuzzy to be useful to you; there will not be enough organization to make all the pieces fit together.

AVOIDING TRAPS

Synthesis presents many traps. Two of the more general ones are using too many elements and expecting convergence. When you get stuck in a synthesis task, ask yourself if you have fallen into one of them. The more you know about these traps, the better able you will be to avoid and get out of them.

Synthesis Trap 1: Too Many Elements

Perhaps the most prevalent trap is trying to put too many elements into a synthesis. If you found many elements of value in your evaluation process, you may be tempted to try to fit them all into the synthesis. This is often a mistake.

A synthesis often improves with the addition of new elements, but there usually comes a point when adding more elements only increases the complexity rather than the value. Past that point, adding elements either doesn't improve the solution or actually makes it worse.

Synthesis Trap 2: Expectation of Convergence

Another trap in the synthesis process is the expectation of convergence, which is the belief that there is one best solution. Often, a problem has more than one useful solution, and sometimes it has many. Finding a useful solution does not necessarily mean finding the "one right answer." Four people working from the same messages on the same synthesis task may come up with four different syntheses—each of which has utility. What do you do in this situation? If you must pick only one, then you need to do an evaluation, this time using the syntheses as the messages and a criterion such as utility. The result of this will be an assessment of the usefulness of the solutions.

What if alternative syntheses all offer the same value? Then you will need to bring in some outside elements. For example, if the syntheses are proposed solutions for a problem and they all are evaluated equally, then you could use an external factor such as cost to break the tie. If each synthesis is equal in terms of what it delivers, then the final decision can be based on resource requirements.

Sometimes it is not possible to compare and evaluate the different products of synthesis, because each is a product of a different type of creative process. For example, suppose four people are asked to produce a synthesis of patriotic messages. The result would convey what patriotism means to Americans. One person synthesizes message elements into a poem. Someone else writes a song. The third person makes a wall mural. The fourth person organizes a rally. All can be high-quality syntheses that incorporate a complex of message elements into a larger message that illustrates the idea of American patriotism. There is no way to make a fair comparison across all four and chose which one is best, because the standards are all different. In this situation, it is best to celebrate the diversity of quality.

This is typically the case in seminars with highly intelligent, motivated, and creative students. As the students work off of the same messages, they each tend to analyze those messages on different dimensions; they construct compare/contrast categories differently and use different criteria for evaluations. Thus they have different materials for their syntheses and different views of what utility means. In a case like this, it is best to appreciate the scholarly and creative efforts and not to force a comparison across the syntheses.

Now that you know the heuristics that can help you with synthesis and how to avoid the traps, please try Exercises 9.1 and 9.2 to practice the skill of synthesis.

EXERCISE 9.1

SYNTHESIZING A PERFECT COLLEGE COURSE

1. List all the college courses you have had so far. If the number is over 10, then cut back your list to only those you have had in the last year or so. If you are new to college, then list about 10 of your favorite high school courses. This is your list of messages to be analyzed.

2. Analyze these courses by listing the characteristics that you liked best about each course. Try to be specific; if you list a general characteristic such as "learned a lot," try to break it down into the specific types of things you learned, such as "learned about myself," "learned how to write better," and so forth. Think about all aspects of the course, such as the material, the professor, the workload, testing, assignments, fellow students, location, time of day, etc.

   When you are finished with this analysis, prepare a sheet of paper for each course, with the course title at the top and the list of characteristics below it.

3. Evaluate the characteristics in each list. Place a star next to the characteristics you valued most. Then, from all the starred items, circle the *most* important one on each sheet.

4. Select the best elements from each analysis. At the top of a fresh sheet of paper, write "My Ideal College Course." List all of the circled items from the lists.

   Try drawing a graphic map of those characteristics. If all the characteristics are the same, then this is simple; draw a big circle and write that characteristic inside the circle. But if there are say three characteristics, then draw three circles and label each one with its characteristic.

Once you have drawn your circles and labeled them with the characteristics, look at the configuration of circles. Should some overlap? If so, re-draw the lines to show this. Perhaps one circle should fit inside another circle. If so, re-draw the lines to show this. Try to capture how you see these characteristics ideally fitting together. You may have to re-draw this graphic several times to get it the way you want it.

Go back to your analysis lists and notice all the starred items—the ones without circles around them. These are important characteristics, but not as important as those characteristics you have already incorporated into your graphic. Now try incorporating the starred items into your graphic. Some of those elements may fit within an existing circle. Other elements may require their own circles; if so, where do those new circles fit?

5. Take a look at the complex whole—your graphic with all its labeled circles. Are there inconsistencies? For example, perhaps you have a major circle labeled "learned a lot" and another major circle labeled "easy workload." These two major characteristics may not be compatible; that is, it may not be realistic to expect to learn a lot from a course with an easy workload.

Work through the inconsistencies. Perhaps a course where you learned a lot only *seems* to have had an easy workload; in actuality the workload may have been large, but you were learning so much that you felt rewarded and the task was not onerous. So perhaps you should re-label "easy workload" as "high rewards for work." This would make the two circles compatible.

As you work through the inconsistencies, you may think of other characteristics to add. Keep adding to, subtracting from, and reconfiguring your graphic until you feel it is useful as a model of your ideal college course. Focus on the criterion of usefulness. Specifically, your resulting graphic should: (a) contain all the characteristics you think are very important, (b) not contain characteristics you would not want, and (c) present a pattern where all characteristics are compatible with one another.

The product of this synthesis is a graphic representation of your ideal college course. You could also express the synthesis in the form of an outline or a narrative. And if you are very creative, you could make the format a syllabus that includes readings, assignments, tests, and so forth.

EXERCISE 9.2

SYNTHESIZING A PERFECT ROMANTIC PARTNER

1. List all the people you have dated romantically. If the number is over 10, then cut back your list to include only those whom you've gone out with for a month or more and thus gotten to know fairly well. This is your list of messages to be analyzed.

2. Analyze those people and relationships. Break each down into components that characterize that person and how you spent your time together.

For the person, think of adjectives (spontaneous, intelligent, athletic, humorous, and so forth). Try to be specific; if you list general characteristics such as "fun," "exciting," and the like, break those down into particular characteristics that made that person fun or exciting.

For how you spent your time, list activities, such as going to the movies, hanging out with friends, talking on the phone, kissing, studying together, and so forth.

Now list the characteristics of how that person treated you. These might include: with respect, with passion, with jealousy, controlling, and so forth.

When you are finished with this analysis, prepare a sheet of paper for each of your romantic partners. Write the person's name at the top and the three lists below (adjectives describing person, how you spent time, and how person treated you).

3. Evaluate the characteristics in each list. Place a star next to those characteristics you valued most in your relationship with that person. Then choose the one starred item that was *most* important to you, and circle it.

4. Select the best elements from each analysis. At the top of a fresh sheet of paper, write "My Ideal Romantic Partner." Copy onto it all the circled items from the lists.

   Try drawing a graphic map of those characteristics. If all the characteristics are the same, then this is simple; draw a big circle and write that characteristic inside the circle. But if there are say three characteristics, then draw three circles and label each one with its characteristic.

   Once you have drawn your circles and labeled them with the characteristics, look at the configuration of circles. Should some overlap? If so, re-draw the lines to show this. Perhaps one circle should fit inside another circle. If so, re-draw the lines to show this. Try to capture how you see these characteristics ideally fitting together. You may have to re-draw this graphic several times to get it the way you want it.

   Go back to your analysis lists and notice all the starred items—the ones without circles around them. These are important characteristics, but not as important as those characteristics you have already incorporated into your graphic. Now try incorporating the starred items into your graphic. Some of those elements may fit within an existing circle. Other elements may require their own circles; if so, where do those new circles fit?

5. Take a look at the complex whole—your graphic with all its labeled circles. Are there inconsistencies? For example, perhaps you have a major circle labeled "spontaneous" and another major circle labeled "dependable." These two major characteristics may not be compatible; that is, it may not be realistic to expect a person to be both spontaneous and a planner whom you can depend upon.

Analyze pairs of major circles that appear to be incompatible. Do they have circles within them? Perhaps the circle labeled "spontaneous" contains several circles inside it labeled "surprises" and "unpredictable." And perhaps the circle labeled "dependable" has several circles inside labeled "plans great dates" and "always know what he/she is thinking." Thus you can see from the components that maybe the two major circles are not so incompatible. At this point, continue to define what you mean by spontaneous and dependable, adding elements to eliminate the inconsistencies so that all the characteristics work together and create a unified whole.

As you work through the inconsistencies, you may think of other characteristics to add. Keep adding to, subtracting from, and reconfiguring your graphic until you feel it is useful as a model of your ideal romantic partner. Thus, the criterion is usefulness. Specifically, your resulting graphic should: (a) contain all the characteristics you think are very important for such a person, (b) not contain characteristics you would not want in such a person, and (c) present a pattern where all characteristics are compatible with one another.

The product of this synthesis is a graphic representation of your ideal romantic partner. You could also express the syntheses in the form of an outline or a narrative. And if you are very creative, you could make the format a drawing of this fantasy person, a poem, or even a song.

CONCLUSION

Synthesis means assembling elements in a fresh, creative manner. The elements are parts of messages that are identified through analysis and subjected to judgment through evaluation. The synthesis can take the form of a new knowledge structure or the transformation of an older knowledge structure. It can also take the form of a new opinion, a new perspective on a situation, or a solution to a problem.

The process of synthesizing follows a three-step algorithm: determine the purpose, select the best elements, and assemble those elements. This chapter provided four heuristics to guide you in working with fixed constraints first, dealing with too many elements, dealing with too few elements, and balancing systematic and creative thinking. It concluded with a caution to avoid the traps of using too many elements and expecting convergence.

CHAPTER 10

Skill 7: Abstracting

LEARNING OBJECTIVES

By reading this chapter, you will:

1. Learn how to develop your skill of abstracting.
2. Understand how to use two heuristics with the skill of abstracting.
   - Comprehending the message
   - Differential challenges in expression
3. Understand how to avoid four traps that can prevent you from using the skill of abstracting well.
   - Over-reduction
   - Partial capture
   - Too much telling; too little showing
   - Not knowing your audience

This chapter and the next deal with skills that are primarily used in sharing knowledge with other people. They are the skills of abstracting and writing persuasively.

Abstracting is the skill of reducing a message down to a shorter version that captures the essence of that message. It requires the ability to make many decisions about which information in the message is central and which is secondary. In order to do this well, you need to recognize the core essence of the message, that is, to filter out the noise in a situation so that the signal is clean and clear.

Abstracting is not merely listing the elements in a message; neither is it rank ordering elements according to their importance. It is more like distilling the essence of the message and communicating it to another person in such a way that the full importance of the message is communicated, but in a much shorter space or time.

The skill of abstracting relies on many of the other skills discussed so far, particularly the skills of analysis, evaluation, and induction. Abstracting requires you to break down the message into parts, then make a judgment about each part as to its importance to the overall message. Abstracting also requires you to look for patterns in the elements and induce a conclusion about the big picture.

A good example of abstracting is news coverage. News organizations continually analyze the events each day and evaluate each of those events. Then they select the most important of those events and put together a package (a newspaper, an evening news program) that is an abstract of the day's events. Each story in that package is itself an abstract, telling you the central essence of an event—the who, what, when, where, and why. For another example, remember the forms you filled out when you were applying to college? They probably asked you to write an essay about something in your life, and they gave you a word (or page) limit. Those essays were exercises in abstracting.

THE ABSTRACTING ALGORITHM

 he abstracting algorithm consists of six steps.

Step 1: Determine Length

Word limit

Maximum number of words allowed in the abstract; you must not exceed this number.

Word target

An ideal number of words to aim for; the abstract can be a little shorter or a little longer.

The first step is to determine how long your abstract is to be. Often the **word limit** is given to you. If the abstract is a class assignment, your professor will give you a word limit or a time limit.

It is very difficult to hit a word or time target exactly. If your word limit is 500 words, it is very difficult to write exactly 500 words and stop, because the stopping point might be in the middle of a sentence. So it is important to make a distinction between a word limit and a **word target.** A word limit is the maximum number of words you can have; a word target is a number that you aim for but that you can go over slightly.

Sometimes you must translate your limit from one form to another. For example, you may be given a class assignment to make an oral report, and your limit is expressed in terms of time (let's say three minutes). But when you write out

The Process of Abstracting

Purpose: To construct a brief, clear accurate description of a message.
Pre-Task: Conduct an analysis to identify message elements.
Process:
1. Determine how long your abstract is to be.
2. Use the results of an evaluation analysis to construct an outline.
3. Create the word budget.
4. Write component sentences.
5. Write an umbrella sentence that conveys the boundaries of the message.
6. Edit the first draft. Use the word budget as a guide.

what you plan to say, you use words. So you must translate words into time. Normal speaking rate is about 200 to 300 words per minute. If you plan to talk rather slowly (but not so slowly as to be noticeable to your audience) and enunciate each word clearly, you should write an abstract of about 600 words for a three-minute oral presentation. If instead your style is to speak fast and with great enthusiasm, you should write an abstract of about 900 words. In the rest of this chapter we will assume that your abstract is in writing, but everything applies to oral abstracts as well.

To translate a word limit into a page limit, figure about 250 words per page. This holds if you are using Courier 12-point font, double spacing, and one-inch margins all around the page.

If you are not given a length limit or target, the best strategy is to keep it as short as possible. It is easier to expand a short abstract than it is to reduce one that is too long. An example of an abstracting task in an informal situation is when your friends ask you to tell them about a movie you just saw. They don't want a long dissertation with lots of detail. Instead, they probably want a few sentences.

Once you know your word limit or word target, you can more efficiently complete the remaining steps.

Step 2: Construct an Outline

The next step is to outline the message you want to abstract. To do this, you need to use the skill of analysis (recall the steps for doing an outline analysis given in Chapter 4). An outline analysis can go many layers in depth, but for abstracting it is best to limit the depth of the outline. If you go to the trouble of constructing an outline with many levels, you will record too much detail, and you will have to ignore most of it when you start writing the abstract. Instead, focus on structure. The structure of the message is much more important than the detail. Ask yourself: Have I captured all the important components in this message, or am I missing an important component? and, Are all the elements I have identified as important components really essential to the message, or have I included some relatively unimportant ones?

Step 3: Create a Word Budget

Now that you have an outline of all the important components from the message that must be reflected in your abstract, you need to assign a word limit or word target to each component so that the sum of the words for the components equals the word limit or target for your total abstract. This is your **word budget.**

When creating the word budget, think about the relative importance of each component. If the components are each equally important, then your word budget should provide the same number of words for each component. However, if one component is much more important, it should be assigned a greater number of words.

The easiest way to approach this task is to use the **balanced technique,** where you divide the words equally among the components in your abstract. For example, let's say your umbrella sentence (see below) is something like: *This book was about the ideas of X, Y, and Z.* Suppose you have 75 more words to use before reaching your limit. In this case, you would use 25 words to develop each of the ideas X, Y, and Z. Thus you are sharing your word budget equally across each of the three ideas. This is the balanced technique.

The balanced technique works well if you regard all three ideas as equally important. However, often one idea is more important than the others. In this case, sharing the word budget equally diminishes the most important idea and elevates the importance of the other ideas; thus you send an inaccurate message to your audience. This works against the purpose of abstracting, which is to convey the essence of the full message as clearly as possible. If you think that three ideas are essential to a message but that the first of the three is more important than the other two, then you should reapportion your 75 words to reflect this. Perhaps the major idea should get 35 words, while the other two essential ideas should get 20 words each.

Step 4: Write Component Sentences

In this step, write a sentence for each major **component** in your outline. Your goal is to capture the essence of that component. At this point, do not worry much about how long each sentence is; instead just try to capture each component in one sentence, even if that sentence is long.

Step 5: Write the Umbrella Sentence

Now that you have written a sentence on each major component, you need to write a sentence that will tie them all together and alert the readers to what is coming. This sentence will become the very first sentence in your abstract.

This is called the **umbrella sentence** because it should cover the entire topic of the abstract. It sets up expectations in the readers' mind and alerts them that certain things will appear in the abstract while other things will not. Thus the umbrella sentence defines the boundaries of what the abstract will cover.

Good umbrella sentences have two characteristics. First, they need to be clear, so that they can alert readers to the topic of the abstract without confusing them. Second, the umbrella sentence must also capture readers' attention and

---

Word budget
A plan for allocating words to different parts of the abstract.

Balanced technique
Apportioning words equally to each component in the outline.

Component sentences
Short sentences that each capture the essence of a component in the message.

Umbrella sentence
The first sentence in the abstract; introduces all components.

make them want to read the rest of your abstract. Therefore, the umbrella sentence should intrigue or stimulate the reader.

Writing the umbrella sentence is typically the most challenging part of writing an abstract. This is because it can be difficult to achieve both clarity and interest in a few words. For example, a very clear umbrella sentence would follow the form of: This abstract is about three ideas: X, Y, and Z. However, this is not a very interesting sentence. To make the sentence much more interesting, you could pose a question. This would engage the readers much more, but it does not clearly tell what the abstract is about. It takes creativity to write a good umbrella sentence that both engages and clearly informs.

Step 6: Edit the First Draft

After you have written your first draft of the abstract, beginning with the umbrella sentence and continuing with a series of component sentences, count the words. You will find one of three situations: the abstract is too long, the abstract is too short, or the abstract is fairly close to the required number of words. In all three situations, you need to edit the first draft to polish it. Your word budget should be a useful guide in your editing.

If the first draft is too long, you will need to cut words. Use the word budget to decide where to cut the words. Which components are over budget? That is, which components have too many words?

If the first draft is too short, you will need to add words. The best way to expand your abstract is to add detail to each component. Perhaps you wrote only one sentence for each component, and now you find you have enough words left to write two sentences for each component. Again, consider whether the balanced technique is the best one to use. Perhaps you will find that your sentences on all but one component are fine in the sense that they each clearly articulate the essence of that component, and you don't need to write more about them. However, maybe one of the other components is unclear or incomplete. In this case, focus your energy on writing more for the weak component.

If your first draft is about the right number of words, then think about whether the balance is good. You might be able to improve your abstract by re-apportioning the number of words for each component. You could sharpen your expression for some components by cutting out words, then add more words on other components that are more complex and require more explanation.

HEURISTICS

The challenge of abstracting is a dual one. First, you have to comprehend the message to some depth in order to understand its essence, that is, its essential parts and their relative importance to the overall message. Second, you need to convey those ideas to someone else. You may be able to do the first task well and envision the message very clearly. However, often the second task is more challenging. This is frequently the case when your understanding of the message takes the form of an image or feeling; translating those things into words can be very difficult. For example, think of a time when someone you felt very strongly for asked you if you loved him or her. You may have been very clear about your feelings in your heart, but translating those feelings into words adequately might have been very difficult. Or perhaps at times an idea has occurred to you in a flash of brilliance—the idea appeared completely formed and in sharp clarity in your mind. But when you tried to explain it to someone else, you found you just could not do it; you kept talking on and on but you knew you were only confusing the other person.

While some images and feelings may require only a few words to communicate clearly, others seem to require thousands of words. This is a common challenge. The two heuristics below can help you deal with this type of challenge.

Abstracting Heuristic 1: Comprehending the Message

If you are finding it difficult to communicate an idea well, the reason might be that you do not really understand it fully, although you might think you do. If you do not comprehend the message well, you cannot abstract it well.

To get started with an abstract, you have to understand what the message really is. This requires a good analysis of the message, and the analysis often must be more than a cognitive one. For example, if the message is a heart-to-heart conversation with a close friend, the analysis needs emotional and perhaps moral elements, because much of the message is not cognitive. If you overlook the other elements in the message, you will fail to comprehend its essence. If the message is a work of art—such as a poem, a film, or a novel—then aesthetic, emotional, and moral elements are likely to be essential to the message.

This is another reason why knowledge structures are so important. For example, if you do not have a good aesthetic knowledge structure for film, then your abstract of a film will lack aesthetic insights, or the aesthetic insights may be faulty. When insights are missing in your understanding, they will certainly also be missing in your abstract.

Abstracting Heuristic 2: Differential Challenges in Expression

Not all ideas require the same number of words to be expressed well. Some ideas can be expressed in a single word that everyone understands; other ideas are more complex and may require you to use hundreds of words to communicate their meaning effectively.

Often, you may follow all the steps in the algorithm and carefully arrive at a logical allocation of words to each component so that you can convey the relative importance of each idea. For example, imagine you are writing a 150-word abstract about four components. Your umbrella sentence is 10 words, and you have allocated the remaining 140 equally among the four components, so that each component gets 35 words. Let's say this works fine for the first three components, but the fourth component is more complex, and there is no way you can describe it adequately in 35 words. Your options are: (a) stay with the 35-word limit for each component and do a poor job communicating the fourth component, or (b) take some words away from the first three components and use them to describe the fourth component. If you choose option (a), your abstract may not be very good; it will fail to communicate the fourth component, and readers will become confused. However, if you choose option (b), then the fourth idea is longer than the others, and this could lead readers to believe that it is far more important than the other components. This is indeed a dilemma; both options present risks. When you are confronted with such a problem, remember your overriding purpose. In constructing an abstract, your goal is to convey the essence of the message to the reader. Thus option (b) is usually better, because it gives you a better opportunity to communicate all of the major ideas clearly.

The ability to share information is directly linked to the ability to put emotions and images into words. To do this at all takes a good deal of skill and a broad vocabulary. When your word budget is very small, skill and vocabulary are even more important.

AVOIDING TRAPS

A good abstract is one that is detailed enough to convey the essence of the important ideas in the message but also broad enough to cover all the essential elements. Hence, abstracting presents two traps. One is to reduce the message down so much that the essence of the message is lost. The other is to focus on only one part of the message and not convey the full essence.

Two additional abstracting traps relate to the importance of considering your audience. Abstracting is a form of communicating, and communicating requires both a sender (writer or speaker) and a receiver (reader or listener). Hence, by considering the needs of the reader, you can be even more effective.

Abstracting Trap 1: Over-Reduction

Let's say you ask your friend to tell you what happened on the last episode of *ER*. Your friend says, "A bunch of doctors helped some sick people." Your friend has captured the essence of the show but has not communicated anything unique about that particular episode. The abstract is too general; it has eliminated so many details that it now fails to convey a vivid sense of what the show was about. Being too concerned about writing as few words as possible can put you in danger of falling into the trap of **over-reduction.**

To illustrate this trap further, let's say the message is a novel of 150,000 words (about 400 printed pages). Think of these 150,000 words as forming the base of a pyramid. As you move up the pyramid, you reduce the number of words. At the very top of the pyramid, the entire book is represented by one word. How far up the pyramid do you need to move to produce a useful abstract? That depends on your purpose in abstracting. Around the 100,000-word level is the region of *Reader's Digest* condensed books. The editors of these condensed novels try to cut out words, paragraphs, and even whole scenes so that the book is much shorter but readers can still follow the plot and understand the characters. Further up the pyramid, the 30,000-word area, is in the region of the Cliff's Notes series. These short paperback books attempt to capture what happens in each chapter and each scene in as few words as possible. At this level, the abstract is no longer really a

Over-reduction

Trap of using too few words and losing the essence of the message.

novel where we see the action unfold and hear the dialog. Instead, the editor tells us what happens rather than showing us. Even further up the pyramid, around the 1,200-word range, is the region of book reports. In about four to six pages, the report describes the novel's events, the characters, and perhaps the theme. At about the 150-word level is the encyclopedia entry range. Near the top of the pyramid, around one to five words, is the title. While the title of a book usually presents its essence, this is usually too few words to be of much use as an abstract. Any message can be abstracted at many different levels, but there is a point beyond which even the most skilled abstracter cannot convey enough elements to give the reader an adequate idea of the message.

To avoid the trap of over-reduction, you need to move past the generality exhibited in an umbrella sentence. The subsequent sentences should give details that make the message vivid.

Abstracting Trap 2: Partial Capture

Partial capture

Trap of focusing on only part of the message and ignoring other parts.

When you feel you cannot capture the full essence of something in the given word allotment, and instead decide to focus on capturing only a small part of the message, you have fallen into the trap of **partial capture.** Returning to the example of your friend telling you about last night's episode of *ER*, let's say your friend tells you, "This mugging victim covered with blood was brought in by an ambulance and the medical team went to work checking his vital signs, then Dr. Carter put a tube down his throat so he could breathe." This abstract provides a lot more vivid detail, but it covers only a few minutes of the hour-long show. It fails to convey what the whole show was about.

Partial abstracts are unsatisfying to listeners, because they are either confusing or they raise questions that they do not answer. One common type of partial abstract is the short blurbs for movies. These serve a marketing purpose by raising questions they don't answer—they get people interested in the movie without giving away the plot. However, an abstract should not tease the reader in this way, because it is not a marketing tool. Instead, abstracting is a tool for communicating the full essence of something clearly and efficiently.

To avoid this trap, it is essential to conduct a component analysis. With this analysis done, you can allocate words to each component and avoid the risk of forgetting about a component or running out of words before you finish describing all components. The word budget will keep you on track by serving as a framework for the abstract and limiting you to a set number of words per component.

Abstracting Trap 3: Too Much Telling; Too Little Showing

The reason why we go to movies, watch TV shows, and read books is to experience the stories—to see and feel the action. We want storytellers to show us what happens, not tell us about it at arm's length. When we watch two characters having an argument, hear their actual words, and watch their faces and body movements, we get more involved in the action than if a storyteller simply says, "Two characters argued." This is the difference between showing and telling.

When you abstract, look out for the trap of only telling about the message. Abstracts communicate much more if you can vividly *show* the essence of the message.

Abstracting Trap 4: Not Knowing Your Audience

With abstracting, each word counts. You cannot waste any of them. To get the most out of each word, you need to know your audience. Avoid words that are unfamiliar to your readers; to achieve clarity you will have to define those words, and that requires you to use more words. Instead, use words with which your readers are familiar, especially words that carry a lot of meaning for them.

Abstracting is a kind of shorthand communication. You try to communicate the essence of big ideas in a few words. Therefore, you need to use words as powerfully as you can. The way to do this is to engage the experience of your readers. For example, think of a conversation you might have with a close friend about an important problem. Because you share a history with your friend, you do not need to use many words to describe the problem. You can get complicated ideas and feelings across with only a few words. Also, a friend may help you clarify things that you are struggling to understand. He or she may say something to you in a sentence or two that will capture your entire problem; your friend has captured the entire essence of what is bothering you in a powerful and succinct way. The communication between friends is very efficient because they share meanings for many words, ideas, images, and feelings, so they can talk in a direct, truncated, short-hand way.

With most abstracting tasks, you do not know your readers personally. You do not have a long history with them. However, you can still think about the knowledge structures they are likely to have. For example, if you are doing an abstract for a class, you have a good idea about your professor's vocabulary, her perspective on the subject matter, and her way of communicating. When you think of shared knowledge structures, you will probably see that you understand your audience better than you thought. When you use that understanding to make the words and ideas in your abstract resonate with your readers, your sentences can be shorter and more powerful while still being clear to your readers.

To practice the skill of abstracting, please try Exercise 10.1.

EXERCISE 10.1

PRACTICE AT ABSTRACTING

1. Read 20 news stories in a newspaper. For each, decide whether or not it is an abstract.

   For each news story, list the ideas introduced in the lead (umbrella) sentence. Then circle and label each of those ideas where it is developed in the rest of the story.

   Are all of the ideas treated equally? If not, why do you think some warranted more words than others?

2. Write an emotional abstract (200 words).

   Choose a person you like and write a 100-word abstract focusing purely on emotions. What is the overriding emotion or set of emotions that define the essence of that person? Write an umbrella sentence to capture the answer to that question, then budget your remaining words to develop each emotion.

   Choose a person you do not like very much and write another 100-word abstract focusing purely on emotions. What is the overriding emotion or set of emotions that the person evokes in you? Write an umbrella sentence to capture the answer to that question, then budget your remaining words to develop each emotion.

3. Write a moral abstract (200 words).

   Choose an ethical issue. It can be a large, national issue, such as prayer in school, abortion, gun control, or privatizing schools, or a personal issue that you are facing.

   Write an abstract, focusing attention on the essence of that issue. Typically ethical issues have at least two sides, so your umbrella sentence should present both sides. Budget your remaining words to develop the main arguments on each side.

   Write another abstract, focusing on your personal belief on the issue. Blend the moral and the emotional. Write an umbrella sentence that presents your position, then budget your remaining words to develop the emotions and reasons to elaborate your position.

4. Write an aesthetic abstract (200 words).

   Choose a movie or television show you have seen recently. Write an abstract about its aesthetic quality. Telling the reader what happened in the show or who the characters were should be in the background; the foreground is your appraisal of the aesthetic quality.

   Write an umbrella sentence to present your strongest aesthetic judgment— what was the best or worst aesthetic element (writing, acting, directing, editing, sound, music, costumes, set designs, special effects, etc.). Budget your remaining words to explain the essence of the quality. For example, if you thought the writing was particularly strong, then you will need to talk about what happened in the plot, but don't present a synopsis of the plot; instead, show why it was such a high-quality story.

5. Write a multidimensional abstract (500 words).

   Think about a novel you have read recently. Think about the events, the characters, the emotions it evoked, the moral dilemmas for the characters, and the quality of the writing. Which of these dominates? That is, in which area do you feel the essence of the book lies?

   Write an umbrella sentence that captures the essence of the book (cognitively, emotionally, morally, and aesthetically). With good novels all these elements are intertwined, but one or two will dominate. Then budget your remaining words to address all four categories (cognitive, emotional, moral, and aesthetic). Show how they are all related. Also, make sure the ideas you express fall under the umbrella sentence.

CONCLUSION

Abstracting is a communication skill by which you capture the essence of a message and create your own new message that is much shorter but that conserves the essence of the original. The chapter gave a six-step algorithm to guide this task. Abstracting tasks are always partially specified. The original message and the word budget are usually specified, but the central essence of the message, its components, and the way to word the abstract are left unspecified and must be determined by you.

This chapter also provided two heuristics for understanding the message and meeting differential challenges in expression. Finally, the chapter gave warnings and solutions for four common traps in abstracting.

Skill 8: Persuasive Expression

LEARNING OBJECTIVES

By reading this chapter, you will:

1. Learn how to develop your skill of persuasive expression.
2. Understand how to use two heuristics with the skill of persuasive expression.

   - Tentative conclusion
   - Hidden thesis

3. Understand how to avoid two traps that can prevent you from using the skill of persuasive expression well.

   - Being satisfied with your first draft
   - Thinking like a writer

Persuasive expression is the skill of presenting a message that a reader can easily accept. Notice that the skill is not simply expression but *persuasive* expression. In essence, all expression is persuasive: the writer wants to persuade readers that what is being expressed is accurate and meaningful. If a message does not persuade readers to start and continue reading, then it has no value; it is not worth reading or writing. So think about the importance of being persuasive when you craft your expressions, whether they be written on paper or delivered orally.

Knowledge does not speak for itself—you must speak for it. When you speak, you have a purpose. If you want people to listen, you must convince them that what you are saying has value to them and that you are providing information that they will find interesting and useful.

THE PERSUASIVE EXPRESSION ALGORITHM

To perform persuasive expression well, you need:

- The ability to understand clearly the conclusion or position you want to argue,
- The ability to select appropriate criteria for the strongest possible argument for your conclusion or position,
- The ability to select the most compelling evidence (positive as well as negative examples) to meet the criteria of your argument,
- The ability to arrange your evidence logically, without gaps,
- The ability to express yourself crisply and clearly.

The algorithm for persuasive expression has seven steps.

Step 1: Identify the Thesis

Thesis

Main point of a persuasive message.

What is it that you want to present or argue? This main point—or **thesis**—is the foundation for your message. When you are clear about your thesis, you have the direction you need to search out relevant evidence to support your arguments.

When your message is about a controversial topic, the thesis statement is easy to construct; it is that in your belief one side of the controversy is correct. Many messages, however, are not about controversial topics, but you can still arrive at a clear thesis by examining your purpose for the message. Let's consider some examples that are not controversial and that might not even seem to be persuasive at all. First, suppose your friend calls and asks what you did last night. You respond with a message that has a persuasive purpose: to convey that you had a great time and he or she really missed out by not coming with you. Or suppose your friend asks you what you thought of a particular movie. You respond with an abstract of the movie, but it has a persuasive purpose: to let your friend know that the movie was bad and he or she should not waste time and money going to it. Or your friend asks you if you like his new haircut—a purple Mohawk with blonde sideburns. You respond with a persuasive message: you want to make him feel

The Skill of Persuasive Expression

Purpose: To articulate clearly the meaning of a message from a point of view, so that the reader will not only understand your interpretation but also agree with it.

Process:

1. Identify the thesis (the conclusion/position you want to argue).
2. Construct a strong set of supporting arguments.
3. Determine the tone.
4. Select the most compelling evidence for each of the supporting arguments.
5. Sequence your arguments and evidence logically and persuasively.
6. Write the first draft.
7. Write a lead that presents your conclusion/position and its supporting argument crisply and clearly.

good (or bad!) about his appearance. Of course, this may test your expression skills to the limit. To meet this challenge, you must keep your purpose clearly in mind.

Step 2: Construct Supporting Arguments

The next step is to think about arguments to support your thesis statement. At this point, do not worry about evidence for your arguments, just list the arguments themselves. Consider what would be your strongest arguments if you could find evidence for them.

Step 3: Determine the Tone

Think about the tone you want to use when making your arguments. Tone has two characteristics: type of appeal and negative/positive.

The appeal can be of three types: logos, ethos, and pathos. **Logos** refers to logic; with a logos appeal, you present evidence that appeals to people's sense of order. You let the facts speak for themselves.

Ethos refers to the credibility of the evidence and the person making the argument. If you are an expert in some area, then your credibility could enhance your arguments. Because of your experience with the topic, people will believe what you say, if you say it forcefully and sincerely.

Pathos refers to the emotions. If you decide to use an emotional tone, think about the emotion you want to stimulate in the reader. If you are writing about a controversial topic, consider evoking emotions of anger and outrage. You could present anecdotes and stories that pull readers into the controversy as they identify with a particular character who is wronged. Skilled writers blend aspects of logos, ethos, and pathos and thereby benefit from the strengths of all three.

Logos
Appeal based on logic and facts.

Ethos
Appeal based on expertise of writer.

Pathos
Appeal based on emotions.

The second aspect of tone is whether your approach is positive or negative. A positive argument provides support for your thesis statement. A negative argument refutes alternative positions. Sometimes speakers are forced to use negative arguments. For example, a person who runs for office with no relevant experience will have to run negative ads that attack the opponent, because as a novice he or she has no record on which to base positive arguments.

If you have a choice, should you use positive or negative arguments? It is best to use a combination of both, especially when the issue is important or when several positions exist on the topic. Negative arguments help you discredit the other positions and inoculate your readers against their appeals. Positive arguments build an affirmative case and help readers feel your position is actually a good one rather than just the least bad of several bad choices.

Step 4: Select Evidence

For each of the supporting arguments, choose the most compelling evidence. First, list all the reasons for supporting it. If your tone is logos, you will need a lot of facts, figures, and quotations from experts. Do your research, then sift through what you have found to select the strongest evidence for each argument.

If your tone is ethos, sift through your experience and select the elements that show you are in fact an expert in this area. Then list your own observations that most strongly support your arguments.

If your tone is pathos, think of how to construct a story that would evoke the emotions you want your readers to have. Create good characters whom the audience can strongly identify with and bad characters they will dislike. Think about how to tell the story so that it is vivid and engaging.

If this is a major project, you will need to do a lot of formal research. Analyze messages in books, articles, Internet content, and your own experiences. Then pass the messages through your filter for relevance—evaluating each to determine which elements are useful for your arguments.

Step 5: Sequence the Arguments

Arrange your arguments and evidence logically and persuasively. To create a meaningful flow, give your readers what they need when they need it. If you raise a question, then answer it as soon as possible. If you leave important questions unanswered, your readers will think your argument has holes.

Imagine that your audience is arguing against you, and consider how readers will respond to your writing. As you present a particular argument, what will the audience's objections be? Try to defuse those objections as quickly and completely as possible. One method is to address their weakest objections first, then build toward dealing with the stronger objections. The advantage of this approach is that it builds momentum early that will take you over the more difficult later sections; the disadvantage is that your audience may become bored with your arguments on the more trivial issues and tune out before you get to your strongest arguments.

Another strategy is to address the audience's strongest objections first. When you have done this, their other objections may evaporate. The more you know about your audience and your topic, the more effectively you will be able to arrange your argument.

Step 6: Write the First Draft

Whether you should prepare an outline before you start writing depends on the project. It is usually more efficient to write from an outline. The time you invest in preparing an outline will pay you back later in fewer rewrites.

If you do not have a clear idea of what you want to say, it may work best simply to start writing. Your purpose may emerge as you write. Craft each component individually without thinking too much about how they will fit together. Once you have the individual components in writing, the order in which the components should appear will become clearer. The disadvantage of this method is that it usually requires more rewriting.

Whether you begin by writing or making an outline, your first draft is never your final draft, unless the message is a very simple one. For important messages, many revisions may be necessary. Each time you revise your draft, you learn more about the topic. The act of writing is a process of discovery. You might discover that some arguments need more research or that the arguments need to be rearranged. You may have to write several drafts before you become really comfortable with the paper. If you get stuck, look at how other people construct arguments, establish their expertise, and appeal to emotions. Use their work as a model for your own arguments.

After several rewrites you may feel that you are going around in circles. Ask yourself, are you really going in circles, or is it an upward **spiral?** As the spiral image suggests, with each new draft you will reach a higher level of understanding. You may be "going around in circles," but you are also gaining a better perspective, and your writing is becoming clearer and clearer.

Spiral
Going back over arguments and evidence with each pass at a higher level of understanding.

When you have produced a draft in which all your arguments seem to be as strong as they can get and are arranged in an effective and interesting sequence, then you are ready to finish the draft with a clear summary. The summary should remind the reader of all the main arguments and bring the message to a powerful conclusion.

Step 7: Write the Lead

The last step is to rewrite the summary as the **lead.** The lead in persuasive expression is like the umbrella sentence in an abstract (see Chapter 10). It clearly defines what the paper is going to show, alerts the reader to the purpose and thesis of the message, and outlines the main arguments that support the thesis. It should also attract the readers' attention and give them a strong reason to read or listen to the full message.

Lead
First sentence of a message; sets up arguments and generates interest.

Many people think of the writing process as if it happened like reading—starting with the first sentence and proceeding in order to the end. This is not usually the best way to write. It is better to write in sections, then assemble them and insert transitions to connect them.

Always write the lead last. During the writing process you will learn a lot more about the topic than you knew when you started. Only when you have finished a good draft are you in a position to write a lead that tells the reader clearly what the message is about. This first paragraph must both grab readers' attention and inform them what to expect in the rest of the message.

The thesis statement should be proportional to your paper. If the total length is only one paragraph, then the lead is the paragraph's topic sentence. If the total length is 10 pages, then the lead may take up the first full page.

Your completed message should begin with a clear statement of your main point, and everything that follows should support that main point. For each important argument, use a subheading to alert your reader to the structure. Each paragraph should have a clear topic sentence, and all the information in each paragraph should support its topic sentence.

HEURISTICS

Persuasive Expression Heuristic 1: Tentative Conclusion

Sometimes you do not know what you want to argue before you begin the process. For example, your professor may assign a term paper and give you a general topic but no clear thesis statement. As you conduct research, you will develop a conclusion about the material. This conclusion becomes your thesis statement.

Researchers frequently begin with a general research question or an area to examine. While they may have some expectations about what they will find, they are open to any conclusion. If they knew all the specifics about what they were going to find ahead of time, there would be no point in conducting the research. It is not until they are well into the research that they begin to see the conclusion or the position they should take.

Tentative conclusion
A conclusion that a writer adopts temporarily and changes until it clearly and accurately reflects the evidence.

Early on in the research, they may come up with a **tentative conclusion.** This can help them summarize and organize what they have done up to that point; it can also guide additional research. However, they must regard such an early conclusion as tentative and keep an open mind as they continue to gather evidence. If all the evidence they gather supports the conclusion, then their confidence in the conclusion grows, and eventually the tentative conclusion is formalized as a thesis statement. If, however, the researcher finds evidence refuting the conclusion, she must use this contrary evidence to synthesize a better conclusion.

Try to view the process as composed of two tasks: the research task and the writing task. The research task can be motivated by a vague question or a broad topic area. The purpose of this task is to find as much information on the topic as possible, then sift through it to arrive at a conclusion. Once you have reached a clear conclusion, you can begin the writing task, which is guided by the conclusion.

Hidden thesis
A thesis that does not appear clearly in the lead; instead readers discover it on their own in the message.

Persuasive Expression Heuristic 2: Hidden Thesis

Although you should almost always express your thesis clearly at the beginning of your message, there are a few situations when this is not advisable and a **hidden thesis** would work better. Hiding your thesis does not mean that it is fuzzy; it should always be very clear to you, and, as the message unfolds, it should become clear to the reader. Hiding the thesis simply means that you do not present it up front but rather let it emerge in the readers' minds as they experience the message.

One reason for hiding your thesis is to avoid coming on too strong. For example, suppose you meet someone whom you want to impress. You would not start your message—which let's say is a conversation—by saying, "I am here to impress you" or "I am a very impressive person." Doing so would probably make the other person feel uncomfortable and make it much harder for you to impress him or her. Instead, you present your arguments so that by the end of the conversation the person clearly gets the point that you are impressive. Your arguments might be your achievements, your conversation style, or stories about yourself that demonstrate your intelligence, compassion, courage, and so forth.

Another reason for hiding your thesis is to make the readers come to believe that the thesis is actually something they thought up themselves. When you accomplish this, not only have you persuaded them to think a certain way, you have gained their commitment, because they think the conclusion was their own idea. Furthermore, they may believe that, because they arrived at the conclusion through logical reasoning, the conclusion is the only reasonable one. If you are able to accomplish this, you have indeed succeeded in being very persuasive!

Hiding your thesis rather than presenting it clearly at the beginning can be an effective technique, but remember that it requires greater skill and should be done only when appropriate.

AVOIDING TRAPS

Persuasive Expression Trap 1: Being Satisfied with Your First Draft

Sometimes you have only a few minutes to compose a message, such as during everyday conversation or in class when you are asked to give an extemporaneous speech or write a 10-minute paper. At these times, the first draft of the message must do. But when you have more time and especially when the message is important to your grade or to your life, you should never be satisfied with the first draft.

The second draft is always better than the first draft, especially when you are very careful in writing the first draft. The more you put into writing an early draft, the more you learn about your topic and how to communicate it.

Even when you prepare an outline before you start writing and follow that outline well, you should still consider your first draft as a draft and not the final product. Put the draft away for a few days, then come back to it. When you read it later, your mind-set will be less like the writer and more like the reader. You will see things in a different context. Even highly skilled writers typically write many drafts.

When you do not begin with an outline, then you must regard the first draft as a process of discovery. Write the first draft not for readers, but for yourself as a way of getting started and putting your thoughts on paper. If you don't enjoy writing, it may be difficult for you to write the first draft knowing that no one will see it. You might feel that you're being made to struggle with a task for which you will get no credit or praise. Try to encourage yourself by thinking about the benefits of writing the first draft. The more you work at it, the stronger your skills will grow, and the struggle will not be as great next time. Also, you cannot write the second draft without having written the first draft. The second draft is almost always much better and easier than the first draft. Think of your reward for writing the first draft as being wrapped up in the grade you get for the final paper.

The rewriting process has two kinds of rewards—external and internal. External rewards are the ones you get from other people. They result from the continual improvement of the message with each draft. With improvements come better grades—external rewards.

Rewriting also provides significant internal rewards. The more you work on improving each draft, the more you strengthen your skill of persuasive expression. The payoff for the effort you put into writing one paper does not end when you get a grade. After that project is over, the challenges of your education continue. Effort you put into any project develops your skills. Knowing you have stronger skills is an internal reward. (Stronger skills bring greater external rewards, as well.)

Try to avoid the trap of cutting corners in order to finish a project quickly. That speed is an advantage only in the short term; it may save you a few hours of work on the one paper, but it does little to help you in the long run. Think of long-term skill development rather than short-term efficiency. Push yourself to do better on each paper, because you are not just working to finish a particular paper; you are also working on developing your skills. Make the effort to analyze and evaluate more messages to provide more and better evidence for your arguments. Write one more draft to sharpen your arguments and clarify your expression. The next time you write a paper, your stronger skills will make it possible for you to earn an even higher grade with perhaps less effort.

Writing tasks do not end at graduation. Throughout your professional career you will be required to create formal messages: reports, proposals, letters, memos, and so forth. The effort you invest in writing papers today will continue to pay off in future papers and writing projects. Each project will get a bit easier to write, if you invest in developing your skills. Avoid the trap of being tempted by short-term efficiency; work hard now and reap the benefits in each successive writing project.

Persuasive Expression Trap 2: Thinking Like a Writer

When you are writing a long paper, you must think like a writer as you make decisions about crafting arguments, incorporating evidence, and arranging information. However, it is a trap to think *only* like a writer. When you have finished putting words on paper, the job is not quite done. When your goal is persuasive expression, you are not finished until you think like a reader.

Examine your paper from the reader's point of view. Try to get inside the reader's mind and ask: Have you presented enough evidence? Is the arrangement effective? Is the argument perfectly clear?

To illustrate this, let's consider an experience you are probably familiar with. Think of the last time you were bothered by a grade you received and went to talk to the professor about it. Your purpose was likely to persuade your professor that the assessment of your performance underestimated your actual learning and that you deserved a higher grade. Students frequently make statements that not only don't help their case, but are actually very damaging. If the students viewed the statements from the professor's point of view, they would probably realize this and take a different approach.

One statement is, "I studied so much for this exam, and it's unfair that you gave me such a poor grade." From the student's point of view, this might be the essence of the problem, but to the professor it has no persuasive value. The professor is likely to think, "If you studied at all and did this badly, your skills must be very weak. I can't tell you to work harder, because you say that you have already worked hard. And you seem so willing to blame *me* and my 'unfair grading' that I don't want to offer to help you improve your skills." Instead, the student could have said something like, "I am a very serious student. I want to do well in your course, but I'm off to a bad start and I need your help. I thought I was well prepared for the test, but apparently I spent all my time studying the wrong things. Could you help me get a better focus on the course?" This type of message is very persuasive to professors. It is much more likely to convince a professor to spend extra time working with you. The professor is not likely to change your grade on the exam you already took, but he will probably take a greater interest in your success on future exams.

A second statement is, "Your grading standards must be unfair, because I have never been given a grade this low before." This statement immediately puts the professor on the defensive, because it blames her for the student's failures. The argument also has no supporting evidence.

A third statement that students often make is, "It doesn't hurt to try to argue for a higher grade." From the student's point of view, this appears to be an innocuous statement. However, from the professor's point of view it appears that the student is saying the professor's time is not worth anything, so the hour spent arguing over the grade has no downside. This is what the professor hears, although it is not usually what the student intends to communicate.

To most professors, grading is a time-consuming, difficult task in which they try to set fair standards and be objective in applying those standards to student work. They have to infer each student's degree of learning from what is on the paper, not from a student's past GPA or time spent studying. If you want to be persuasive, you must understand the task from the professor's point of view and argue from there.

The general principle is to get inside the readers' minds. Try to see the topic from that perspective, then use the readers' values, rhythms of expression, and ways of thinking to communicate with them. By so doing, you minimize the barriers to communication. What you say will be clearer; it can also resonate with the readers' own values. This doesn't mean that you *adopt* those values, just that you accept that the readers hold them. Getting into the professor's world does not necessarily mean that you agree with his views, only that you get into the world of scholarship—and demonstrate that you are a strategic thinker.

To practice the skill of persuasive expression, please try Exercise 11.1.

EXERCISE 11.1

PRACTICE AT PERSUASIVE EXPRESSION

The exercises in this chapter parallel the exercises in the chapter on abstracting. Whereas the challenge in the abstracting exercises was to boil the essence of a message down to a limited number of words, the challenge in these exercises is to present a point of view and arguments that the reader will accept.

1. Read several editorials and letters to the editor in a newspaper. Do an outline analysis of each.

   Which of the messages are most persuasive? What key characteristics are shared by those messages you regard as being persuasive? Do you see any patterns in the elements of the messages you regard as not persuasive? Can you write a general rule for what it takes to be persuasive?

2. Write an emotional argument.

   Choose a person you like and analyze why that person makes you feel good. Write an outline organizing the qualities of that person that make you feel good.

   Now think of a friend who does not know that person. Imagine calling your friend and telling him or her about this person who makes you feel good. Your goal is to persuade your friend to feel good about this person. Get inside the mind and heart of your friend and rewrite your outline so that your presentation will be persuasive.

3. Make a moral argument.

   Choose an ethical issue. It can be a large, national issue, such as prayer in school, abortion, gun control, or privatizing schools. Or it can be a personal issue that you are facing.

   Write an outline for an argument supporting your position on the issue. Use that outline to talk about the issue with someone who agrees with you.

   Now think about a person who would not agree with you on this issue, and use your outline to talk about the issue with this person. How would you change your outline to restructure your presentation?

4. Make an aesthetic argument.

   Choose a movie or TV genre you like (examples include action/adventure, romantic comedy, musical, crime drama, cartoon, science fiction). Write an outline of the aesthetic qualities (types of themes, characters, plots, settings, etc.) of shows in that genre. Use the outline to make a presentation to someone who likes the same genre.

   Find a person who hates that genre. Use your outline to try to persuade that person of the virtues of that genre. How would you change your outline to restructure your presentation?

5. Find a paper you wrote for another class, preferably one that you have not read in at least three months and that did not receive a high grade.

What is the thesis of this paper?

Do an outline analysis on your paper.

Now think about the topic and write an outline that you would use if you wrote the paper now. Try to construct an outline with about five main points. If your previous paper had fewer than five main points, then think about creating new major lines of argument to support your thesis. If your previous outline had more than five major points, could you reorganize it to put some of those points under other major points?

Elaborate your new outline by thinking of ways to make each line of argument stronger. What additional facts could you work in, and what sources of information could you check to locate those facts? Are there quotations from experts that would strengthen your arguments? If your outline is dominated by cognitive information, can you work in emotional, moral, and aesthetic information to increase the persuasive appeal?

Now that you have a more elaborate outline, should you re-frame your thesis statement?

Think about a professor in one of your current classes. How would you change this paper to make it acceptable to that professor's expectations? Rework your outline.

CONCLUSION

All good expression is persuasive. When you write or speak, you should present a point of view clearly so that readers or listeners can understand and appreciate the knowledge you are conveying. They should feel that they are receiving value for their time.

A seven-step algorithm can help you apply the skill of persuasive expression. However, each message has its own special challenges, so heuristics are also helpful as guides. This chapter presented two heuristics: dealing with tentative conclusions and using a hidden thesis. This chapter also warns you about two traps: being satisfied with your first draft and only thinking like a writer.

Springboard 12

LEARNING OBJECTIVE

By reading this chapter, you will learn how to continue developing your
skills as a strategic thinker.

Congratulations! You have made it all the way to the last chapter. By this point, you should have a good idea of what a strategic thinker is and how to become one yourself.

This book is about to end, but your journey is just beginning. You can use the ideas in this book to get more out of any message and to do more with all kinds information. The more you use the strategic thinking perspective, the more you will be able to get out of your college courses—regardless of their content. As a strategic thinker, you can improve your performance in the physical sciences, the social sciences, the arts, the humanities, and professionally oriented courses, because you have developed a set of general skills that are valuable in all departments. As a strategic thinker, you will do better in introductory courses, because you know how to make sense of new bodies of information. You will also do better in advanced courses, because you have developed stronger knowledge structures that organize the new material much more efficiently. Furthermore, as a strategic thinker you will be able to make better decisions throughout your life, because you will be able to locate information more efficiently and use it more effectively every day.

This last chapter is really a pep talk. Here are a dozen ideas that can help you keep thinking strategically.

1. Develop Your Skills

Whatever your current skill levels are, you can raise them substantially. Skills are like muscles. With exercise, you get stronger.

The eight skills work together just as the muscles in your body work together, so it is important that you build strength in all of these skills to keep them balanced. You need to be confident in all eight skills in order to be a strong strategic thinker.

Every person is born with a different set of innate abilities, some of them stronger than others. All of these abilities, even the strongest, can still be strengthened. Life is a process of change, and you can improve your skill levels with the right exercises.

2. Take Control

You have attained your current level of thinking skills through a combination of factors that include your innate abilities, maturation, conditioning, and work. Much of your development has been guided by teachers in elementary school through high school. Those teachers focused primarily on helping you develop fundamental skills of reading, arithmetic, listening, descriptive writing, and the like. These skills can help you most with fully specified problems.

Now that you are in higher education, almost all of the challenges you will face in your courses—especially beyond the introductory level—will be partially specified problems. To meet this type of challenge, you must take control of your thinking process. Think for yourself and be creative as you work your way through these challenges. Don't depend on other people to tell you what to do, because then they will be controlling what you do and think. Imagine your education as a car; professors and books can show you *how* to drive, but they should not control *where* you drive. Look for guidance in becoming a strategic thinker, but then use the skills you have learned to think for yourself.

3. Develop All Your Thinking Skills

As a strategic thinker, you need a balanced set of skills. If you feel that a few of your skills are weaker than others—and most of us do feel this way—then do not ignore those weaknesses by trying to work around them. Instead, work *most* on them. If your right ankle is weak, you may be tempted to baby it and not put much weight on it. However, the longer you baby your ankle, the weaker it will get. Your left leg will need to get stronger in order to do more of the work of walking. This might be acceptable in the short term, but over the long term, you will develop a limp and your posture will suffer. You are then likely to develop problems in other muscle groups, and your entire well-being can be compromised. It is far better to recognize weaknesses early and overcome them than to ignore them.

4. Remember, Knowledge Is More Important than Facts

In our information-rich culture, getting access to facts is easy. The overriding challenge now is to create knowledge for yourself. You do this by using your tool skills to sort through the information and filter in only the accurate and useful facts. Then you must look for patterns across those facts and continually reconfigure those facts in your knowledge structures.

Today, it is impossible for anyone to keep up with the flow of information. According to Limerick (1992), in 1700 an educated person in Western Europe could actually read everything that was worth reading, but by 1800 the amount of information had increased beyond an educated person's ability to consume it all. As of 1900, a person could keep up with a particular field of human inquiry, such as law, medicine, or physics. By the late 1900s, however, mastery of the total set of information in all but the narrowest of fields was no longer realistic. Now the only way to avoid getting drowned by all the messages and instead succeed as a professional is to make filtering decisions efficiently and construct meaning effectively.

Remember too that information changes quickly. Even if you do learn many facts in college, most of those facts will be outdated within a few years after you graduate. Facts decrease in value over time; what increases in value over time is a good set of knowledge structures. These provide the context for you to use in constructing meaning out of new facts.

5. Use Your Education to Strengthen Skills and Develop Knowledge Structures

Ask yourself if you are getting enough breadth and depth in your curriculum and courses. At most colleges, students achieve breadth through distribution requirements usually taken during the first two years of college. These courses push you to try a wide range of different forms of thinking. The courses for your major provide depth.

Although many students think that majoring in a particular subject is good preparation for a career, that is shortsighted. If you are serious about preparing for a challenging professional career, you should take a broad perspective on your future. This means developing a set of skills that you can use in any situation in any professional career.

A major in college shows you the value of in-depth context. When you also have a broad context, you are in a much better position to understand anything that may happen to you in the future and to make decisions more successfully and confidently. Ask yourself how broad your education is (see Exercise 12.1).

EXERCISE 12.1

THINKING ABOUT A PLAN FOR REAL-WORLD KNOWLEDGE

Make an assessment of your knowledge structures of the world.

Start with a template of knowledge, such as the headings *Arts*, *Humanities*, *Social Sciences*, and *Physical Sciences*. Then fill in the knowledge areas under each by looking at your college catalog's list of academic departments and courses. You could also go to the library and look at how knowledge is organized there either by the Dewey Decimal system or the Library of Congress system. Sketch a set of blocks to represent the areas of knowledge. The big blocks (such as *Physical Science*) should be composed of smaller blocks (such as *Physics, Chemistry, Biology*, etc.). Some of these smaller blocks (such as *Biology*) may also be composed of subsets (such as *Botany* and *Zoology*). Try to create a picture of how human knowledge is generally organized.

Think back over the last two years. What significant learning experiences have you had during that time? A significant learning experience is something you remember as valuable to your learning, such as:

- A course that challenged you and made you think.
- An interest in something that motivated you to read a series of books (or search out information in other media) and discuss the issues.

Write these significant learning experiences in the appropriate content blocks in your template in red ink.

What learning experiences have you had over the last two years that were "just okay"? These might be courses where you learned something but not a whole lot, or minor interests that led you to read about a topic, but not in depth. Write these significant learning experiences in the appropriate content blocks in your template in blue ink.

Look at the patterns on your template.

Where are the blank areas with no red or blue ink? Have you been broadening your knowledge, or have you been playing it safe and avoiding new areas? What does this tell you about what you value in a college education and the kind of person you want to become as a graduate?

Where are the red areas? Are they all in one part of the template or are they sprinkled all over? What does this pattern say about you as a learner and what it takes to make something a significant learning experience?

Where are the blue areas? What do these have in common? How do the blue areas differ from the red areas? To what extent were these experiences less than optimal because of outside forces (such as the teacher, the course materials, etc.) or because of something within you (such as motivation, previous knowledge structures, etc.)? What does this tell you about yourself as a learner?

Think about your overall goals for learning.

Do you have goals for depth? Are you building elaborate knowledge structures in a few particular areas to create a foundation for a career or further study?

Do you have goals for breadth? Are you building knowledge structures across a variety of areas so you have contexts for a wide range of topics?

College courses are valuable when they provide lots of information on a topic and guide you to create strong knowledge structures. However, these knowledge structures, no matter how elaborate, are still only the beginning of life-long learning. You will likely encounter information on the topic throughout your life, and you will continually need to make decisions about using that information to update your knowledge structures. After you have graduated, you will have an even greater need to be a strategic thinker. As much information as you encounter in college, you will find much more in the real world.

6. Cultivate Both Talents Needed for Strategic Thinking

One talent is logical thinking, which requires you to follow rules carefully and systematically. This demands discipline in following algorithms and crystalline intelligence for acquiring them. Algorithms are rules that have been developed over millennia of human thinking and problem solving. Applying these algorithms gives your thinking structure and clarity.

Remember that these rules are not specific enough to meet every situation. To be a complete strategic thinker, you also need the second talent, creative or lateral thinking. This talent is necessary because the rules will rarely get you all the way to a solution. Some leap of thought is usually needed. Creativity and insight enhance your thinking process.

The algorithms can get you started, but you also need heuristics to help you work through the places along the problem-solving path where the algorithms cannot guide you. Heuristics are especially important in solving partially specified problems.

7. Remember that Skills Are Tools

Be careful not to spend all your time developing skills for their own sake. If you do, you will undoubtedly fall into one of two traps. One is the "medieval scholar" trap: you work on skills for the sake of showing off and get into lots of discussions about theoretical questions like how many angels can dance on the head of a pin. Such discussions can be interesting mental calisthenics from time to time, but when they become a way of life, you are trapped. Be careful not to work out your mental muscles to the point of becoming musclebound—spending all your time developing muscles just for the sake of having muscles and eventually finding yourself unable to use them for any useful work.

The other trap is "I'm not good enough yet." People who are stuck in this trap work very hard on their skills but never feel they have reached competence, so they never feel good about their achievement. Don't be like a person who goes to the hardware store every day to buy new tools, but never actually uses the tools to make anything, because she does not feel competent to use all those tools. You cannot wait to become an expert at using a hammer before you allow yourself to use the hammer. Thinking like this is a trap. Skills are tools. You can only learn to use them by actually using them.

You have probably heard the saying that practice makes perfect. With skill development, this does not hold, because we can never reach perfection—such a goal is unrealistic. However, practice does make better, and the more practice the "more better."

8. Have Goals to Guide Your Thinking

Thinking is not an end in itself but a tool for achieving goals. Therefore building skills should take place within a goal-directed perspective. When you have goals for your life, skills become valuable as a means for achieving those goals.

The expectation of reaching goals can sustain you when the process is very challenging. A vision of who you are and what you want to become can make the effort of skill development meaningful.

Your goals may not be specific, such as earning a 3.8 GPA and gaining admission to medical school. More than likely your most important goals will be more abstract, such as:

- To lead an interesting and productive life.
- To find challenges of all kinds and excel at meeting them.
- To understand more about the world and my place in it.

People who have no goals tend to approach problems from an efficiency point of view. They use skills in a "quick and dirty" manner to reach some sort of solution as quickly as possible. If efficiency is the goal driving your problem solving, then your skills will not be challenged and will not develop.

Accuracy is the goal that will lead you to challenge and develop your skills. On rare occasions it will be possible to achieve both accuracy and efficiency, but typically you must choose one or the other. The more you are motivated by efficiency and making quick judgments, the less likely you will be to achieve accuracy in those judgments. In situations where you must make many judgments in a short period of time or where the consequences of inaccuracy are minor, efficiency is the most appropriate goal. When you are faced with a very important decision or when you want to do quality scholarly work, accuracy is an essential goal.

9. Translate Goals into Objectives

Keep in mind that goals are usually very general and long term. This keeps us focused on the big picture. However, general goals can also seem overwhelming, because they are ambitious and take a long time to attain. It helps to translate your general goals into specific, more easily achievable objectives. These objectives become the markers along the journey to your goals, providing guidance and direction.

Specific objectives are easier to achieve than are general goals. Each time you achieve an objective, you feel a sense of accomplishment that helps keep you motivated on the path to your bigger goals.

10. Commit to Investing in Your Future

The earlier you start investing time and energy, the greater the payoff will be. But don't expect a linear relationship between the amount of effort you put in and the amount of payoff you will get. With a linear relationship, you get one unit of output for each unit of input. For example, if you work at a job that pays $10 per hour and you work one hour, you expect to be paid $10—one unit of work (an hour) translates into one unit of pay (the hourly rate). If you put two units in, you expect two units out. Linear thinking suggests that for each unit of effort you put into a task, you should get one unit of return. If you work 10 hours, you expect to be paid $100; if instead you are paid $80, that seems unfair.

It is a mistake to expect a linear relationship between the effort you make to become a strategic thinker and the benefits you will gain. If you make this mistake, you will greatly *overestimate* the return you will get immediately and greatly *underestimate* the return you will get in the long term. Instead, you should set your expectations by the learning curve (see Figure 12.1).

The learning curve shows the relationship between effort and return. When you are strengthening skills, the "effort" is your hours of study or amount of concentration, and the "return" is strength. The straight dotted line indicates a linear relationship, and the solid line illustrates the learning curve. Let's take a closer look at the learning curve. As the line moves right (more units of effort), it does not move up (units of output) very much at first. This means that when

Figure 12.1 Learning curve.

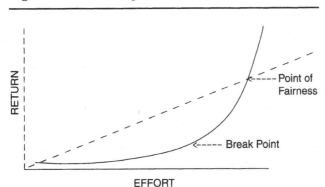

your skill level is low, it takes a lot of effort to get it to move up much. You keep putting in effort, but you don't get much return. However, if you continue putting in effort, you will eventually reach the "break point," where the returns start to increase.

Most people quit before they reach the break point. Why? They are trapped by linear thinking. They have not been gaining much strength for the amount of effort, and they think that this will continue to be the case. They conclude that they will always have to work hard for very little gain, so they quit.

What these individuals do not realize is that if they stick to the task, they will eventually reach the break point and begin to get greater returns on their effort. In the early stages of a task, you are simply "paying your dues" and not receiving much in return. During this time you must have faith that your hard work will eventually pay off. Furthermore, you will eventually reach the "point of fairness," where you will have received a reward equal to the effort you made.

If you can stick it out through the early phase and reach the break point, then everything becomes easier and you will start to feel that the process is fun. Remember when you learned to ride a bicycle? The first few days were probably very frustrating, because you would practice and practice but not seem to get better. You might have seen so little improvement that you wondered if you would ever be able to ride without training wheels. Then one day you suddenly "got it." You were riding by yourself, and it felt so good you couldn't stop smiling! After that you learned more very quickly: how to go faster and to maneuver around obstacles. Before long you may even have been showing off—riding with no hands or standing on your seat. You managed to get past the early frustration, when you made little progress for lots of effort. But once you started experiencing success, it came very rapidly. Eventually you got to the point where riding a bike seemed to take no effort at all.

The most rewarding part of the learning curve is beyond the point of fairness, where you get back more than you put in. In this area, you appear to be doing things with little effort, while achieving more success than other people who are working much harder. Those struggling people may look at you and think: "If she/he can do it so easily, why can't I? What is wrong with me?" What is wrong with them is that they are thinking linearly. Many people do not understand the relationship between effort and reward, so they do not make it to the break point.

One more thing about the learning curve in Figure 12.1. As shown, it is a smooth line, with no bumps. However, if we could plot the actual relationship for a particular person, the line would not be smooth—it would have lots of little bumps and dips along the way. Think of a roadmap of the United States, where the interstate highways are shown as relatively straight lines. In reality, they bend and turn as they swing around hills and follow rivers. When you exercise your thinking muscles, you will have some days when nothing will go right and other days when things will go better than expected. It is important to keep in mind the bigger picture, the overall pattern of the learning curve.

Think of learning to be a strategic thinker as requiring an investment over a long period of time—an investment that will pay compound interest. Money invested in an account with compound interest grows fast, because last year's interest becomes part of this year's principle. Each year the interest becomes larger as the base continues to grow. The same is true of efforts invested in becoming a strategic thinker. The payoff this year may be relatively small, but that effort will help make your knowledge style stronger next year. If you keep investing your efforts, the base will continue to grow larger, so each year the same effort will pay off more. The key to making this work for you is to get started early, and invest effort now. Don't expect huge returns immediately—but trust that they will come later.

11. Continually Challenge Things

Don't accept things as they appear on the surface. Analyze them—dig below the surface to understand how things really work. Don't automatically accept other people's evaluations, groupings, inductions, deductions, or syntheses. Work things through for yourself. If your skills are strong, you will likely be able to do these things better for yourself. You will be using the thinking skills to serve your own goals, so the products of your efforts will fit much better into your own knowledge structures.

Challenge yourself:

- Don't be satisfied with your current knowledge style. Try to improve your traits.
- Don't be satisfied with your current levels of skills. You can make them stronger and become a more powerful strategic thinker.
- Don't be satisfied with your existing knowledge structures. They may contain facts that are out of date or faulty. They may also be too limited; you always need more information.

When you continually challenge information and yourself, you strengthen your skills and broaden your knowledge structures, becoming a more powerful strategic thinker. When you think more powerfully, you get much more in return for your effort. The rewards are great: you are able to figure things out better, see more connections, develop better and more creative solutions to problems, and explain your thinking to other people clearly and persuasively.

12. Have Fun!

You have read about lots of reasons to be a strategic thinker. As you close this book, here is a final, and perhaps the simplest, reason for becoming a strategic thinker: Because it is fun! When you can transform information in all sorts of powerful ways, you can make your mark on other people and on the world. Now, go out and see how much fun you can have!

Pep Talk

1. Develop your skills.
2. Take control.
3. Develop all your thinking skills.
4. Remember, knowledge is more important than facts.
5. Use your college education to strengthen your skills and develop your knowledge structures.
6. Cultivate both talents needed for strategic thinking.
7. Remember that skills are tools.
8. Have goals to guide your thinking.
9. Translate goals into objectives.
10. Commit to investing in your future.
11. Continually challenge things.
12. Have fun!

References

Adler, Mortimer J. (1940). *How to Read a Book: The Art of Getting a Liberal Education.* New York: Clarion.

Anderson, J. R. (1985). *Cognitive Psychology.* New York: W. H. Freeman.

Applebee, A. (1981). *Writing in the Secondary School: English and the Content Areas.* Urbana, IL: National Council of Teachers of English.

Applebee, A. (1984). Writing and reasoning. *Review of Educational Research, 54,* 577–596.

Bareiss, R. (1989). *Exemplar-Based Knowledge Acquisition: A Unified Approach to Concept Representation, Classification, and Learning.* Boston: Academic Press.

Berger, P. L., & Luckmann, T. (1966). *The Social Construction of Reality.* Garden City, NY: Doubleday & Company.

Bloom, A. (1987). *The Closing of the American Mind.* New York: Simon and Schuster.

Bloom, B. S. (Ed.). (1979). *Taxonomy of Educational Objectives: The Classification of Educational Goals. Book 1: Cognitive Domain.* New York: David McKay Company.

de Bono, E. (1970). *Lateral Thinking: Creativity Step by Step.* New York: Harper & Row.

de Bono, E. (1968). *New Think: The Use of Lateral Thinking in the Generation of New Ideas.* New York: Basic Books.

Boyer, E. (1983). *High School: A Report on Secondary Education in America.* Princeton, NJ: Carnegie Foundation for the Advancement of Teaching.

Browne, M. N., & Keeley, S. M. (2001). *Asking the Right Questions: A Guide to Critical Thinking* (6th ed.). Upper Saddle River, NJ: Prentice Hall.

Bruner, Jerome S. (1960). *The Process of Education.* Cambridge, MA: Harvard University Press.

Cattell, R. B. (1963). Theory of fluid and crystallized intelligence: A critical experiment. *Journal of Educational Psychology, 54,* 1–22.

Churchman, C. W. (1971). *The Design of Inquiring Systems: Basic Concepts of Systems and Organizations.* New York: Basic Books.

Clifford, G. (1984). Buch un lessen: Historical perspectives on literacy and schooling. *Review of Educational Research, 54,* 472–500.

D'Souza, D. (1991). *Illiberal Education: The Politics of Race and Sex on Campus.* New York: The Free Press.

Emanuel, R., & Potter, W. J. (1992). Do students style preferences differ by grade level, orientation toward college, and academic major? *Research in Higher Education, 33,* 395–414.

Ennis, R. H. (1987). A taxonomy of critical thinking dispositions and abilities. In J. B. Baron & R. J. Sternberg (Eds.), *Teaching Thinking Skills: Theory and Practice* (pp. 9–26). New York: Freeman.

Ennis, R. H. (1992). The problem of skills versus content. In R. A. Talaska (Ed.), *Critical Reasoning in Contemporary Culture* (pp. 5–27). Albany, NY: State University of New York Press.

Forbes, R., & Brown, R. (1981). *Reading, Thinking, and Writing.* Denver: National Assessment of Educational Progress.

Forsberg, G. E. (1993). *Critical Thinking in an Image World: Alfred Korzybski's Theoretical Principles Extended to Critical Television Evaluation.* Lanham, MD: University Press of America.

Gibbs, R. W. (1995). *The Poetics of Mind: Figurative Thought, Language, and Understanding.* Cambridge: Cambridge University Press.

Goleman, D. (1995). *Emotional Intelligence.* New York: Bantam Books.

Goodlad, J. (1983). *A Place Called School: Prospects for the Future.* New York: McGraw-Hill.

Grant, G. E. (1988). *Teaching Critical Thinking.* New York: Praeger.

Haney, W. (1984). Testing reasoning and reasoning about testing. *Review of Educational Research, 54,* 597–654.

Healy, J. M. (1990). *Endangered Minds: Why Children Don't Think and What We Can Do About It.* New York: Simon & Schuster.

Hirsch, E. D., Jr. (1987). *Cultural Literacy: What Every American Needs to Know.* Boston: Houghton Mifflin.

Hirsch, E. D., Jr., Kett, J. F., & Trefil, J. (1993). *The Dictionary of Cultural Literacy* (2nd ed.). Boston: Houghton Mifflin.

Johnson, R. H. (1992). The problem of defining critical thinking. In S. P. Norris (Ed.), *The Generalizability of Critical Thinking: Multiple Perspectives on an Educational Ideal* (pp. 38–53). New York: Teachers College Press.

King, P. M. (1986). Formal reasoning in adults: A review and critique. In R. A. Mines & K. S. Kitchener (Eds.), *Adult Cognitive Development: Methods and Models* (pp. 1–21). New York: Praeger.

Kitchenor, K. S. (1983). Cognition, metacognition and epistemic cognition: A three-level model of cognitive processing. *Human Development, 4,* 222–232.

Large, P. (1984). *The Micro Revolution Revisited.* Totowa, NJ: Rowman & Allanheld.

Leary, D. (Ed.). (1990). *Metaphors in the History of Psychology.* New York: Cambridge University Press.

Limerick, P. (1992, July). Point of view. *The Chronicle of Higher Education,* p. A32.

Lipman, M. (1988). Critical thinking: What can it be? *Analytic Teaching, 8,* 5–12.

Lyman, P., & Varian, H. R. (2001, Nov. 6). *How Much Information, 2000.* Retrieved from www.sims.berkeley.edu/how-much-info.

Matthews, J. (1992, April 13). To yank or not to yank? *Newsweek,* p. 59.

Mayer, R. E. (1992). *Thinking, Problem Solving, Cognition.* New York: W. H. Freeman and Company.

McPeck, J. E. (1981). *Critical Thinking and Education.* Oxford: Martin Robinson.

Mines, R. A., & Kitchener, K. S. (1986). *Adult Cognitive Development: Methods and Models.* New York: Praeger.

Naisbitt, J. (1984). *Megatrends: Ten New Directions Transforming Our Lives.* New York: Warner Books.

Neimark, E. D. (1979). Current status of formal operations research. *Human Development, 22,* 60–67.

Newell, A., & Simon, H. A. (1972). *Human Problem Solving.* Englewood Cliffs, NJ: Prentice Hall.

Norris, S. P. (Ed.). (1992). *The Generalizability of Critical Thinking: Multiple Perspectives on an Educational Ideal.* New York: Teachers College Press.

Nosich, G. M. (2001). *Learning to Think Things Through: A Guide to Critical Thinking in the Curriculum.* Upper Saddle River, NJ: Prentice Hall.

O'Keefe, V. (1999). *Developing Critical Thinking: The Speaking/Listening Connection.* Portsmouth, NH: Boynton/Cook.

Paul, R. (1990). *Critical Thinking.* Rohnert Park, CA: Center for Critical Thinking and Moral Critique.

Paul, R. W. (1982). Teaching critical thinking in the strong sense: A focus on self-deception, world views, and a dialectical mode of analysis. *Informal Logic Newsletter, 4*(2), 2–7.

Perkins, D. (1992). *Smart Schools: From Training Memories to Training Minds.* New York: Free Press.

Pinker, S. (1997). *How the Mind Works.* New York: W. W. Norton & Company, p. 26.

Polya, G. (1957). *How to Solve It* (2nd ed.). Princeton, NJ: Princeton University Press.

Potter, W. J., & Clark, G. (1991). Styles in mass media classrooms. *Feedback, 32*(1), 8–11, 24.

Potter, W. J., & Emanuel, R. (1990). Students' preferences for communication styles and their relationship to achievement. *Communication Education, 39,* 234–249.

Pulaski, M. A. S. (1980). *Understanding Piaget: An Introduction to Children's Cognitive Development* (revised and expanded edition). New York: Harper & Row.

Reeves, W. W. (1996). *Cognition and Complexity: The Cognitive Science of Managing Complexity.* Lanham, MD: Scarecrow Press.

Sizer, T. (1984). *Horace's Compromise: The Dilemma of the American High School.* Boston: Houghton Mifflin.

Wurman, R. S. (1989). *Information Anxiety.* New York: Doubleday.

Index